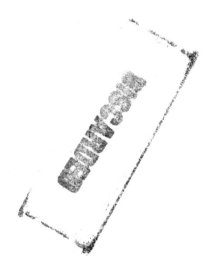

IAN McKAY

THE CRAFT TRANSFORMED

An Essay on The Carpenters of Halifax, 1885-1985

Halifax *Holdfast Press* 1985

ISBN 0-9692117-0-8

Typeset and printed in the Maritimes by union labour. ®

Canadian Cataloguing in Publication Data

McKay, Ian, 1953-
    The Craft Transformed

1. United Brotherhood of Carpenters and Joiners of America. Local 83 (Halifax, N.S.) - History. 2.Trade-unions - Carpenters -_Nova Scotia - Halifax - History. I. Title

HD6528.C32U534 1985   331.88'194   C85-099297-4

Distributed by Formac Publishing Company Limited
5359 Inglis Street
Halifax, Nova Scotia
B3J 2A1

Contents

Preface

This book has been written to mark the centenary of Local 83 of the United Brotherhood of Carpenters and Joiners of America. Besides sustaining me for a year, Local 83 has generously given me office space and free access to their superb archive of labour records. These minute books, ledgers, and other records constitute the basic source for this study. Stretching from 1888 to 1985 (but with a bothersome gap between 1913 and 1927), Local 83's records are a treasure for Canadian labour historians which, I hope, will be preserved in the public archives and used by those interested in all facets of our labour and civic history. Although the union has commissioned this volume, it has not imposed any restrictions on how I have approached the history of the Halifax carpenters. I thank Local 83 for the help it has given me, and I hope this portrait of the Halifax carpenters will serve as a useful contribution to their centennial celebrations.

At the same time, I hope my essay will prompt reflection on the broad theme of the place of work in our society, for its main theme is the efforts of skilled craftsmen to defend their economic and social position in a century of rapid change. Four eras stand out in the history of this craft. From the eighteenth century to the mid-nineteenth century master craftsmen, journeymen, and apprentices regulated the craft, not without conflict, but without any sense of an entrenched conflict between masters and men. Then from the 1860s to the end of the nineteenth century, the first period to be covered in detail in this study, journeymen and masters began to see themselves as having different and potentially clashing interests in the construction industry, as the old master craftsmen gradually ceded pride of place to general contractors and speculative builders. But this change was less radical than the shift which opened the third period of the history of the craft. Large, diversified, outside construction companies transformed the whole world of the Halifax carpenters, destabilizing the labour market and intensifying production in the early years of this century. Finally, a fourth period was born in the 1920s and is still with us today. Representing just as radical a shift in direction as the previous transition, this period entailed the increasing regulation of the construction industry by the state, and the assumption by the trade union of semi-public functions in the control of the labour market. This short essay explores these periods and shifts in direction, but without presenting itself as a definitive work on a craft and a process which both deserve much additional scholarly work.

"Compared with that of a barrister," R.H. Tawney, the British historian, wrote in 1918, "the work of building a house, or extracting coal, or manufacturing cotton piece-goods, is a school of morals. It is certainly no meaner in itself than is that of attending the sick or instructing the ignorant. It is as necessary, and therefore it is as honourable."[1] Few workers can make so plausible a claim to be indispensable as those carpenters who help to build the very houses, offices and factories in which we live, and few (save, perhaps, the coal miners) have faced the same daunting problems of chaos induced by the business cycle, the same savage competition in the labour market, and the same difficulty in defending their status as skilled workers. The history of Local 83, and of the craftsmen it has represented, tells us much about the city of Halifax and the people who actually built it, but it also shows us the harsh world of work as it has been transformed and transformed again in capitalist society.

My aim has been to write a solidly researched historical essay for a trade union, and this has led to two important changes in normal academic style. First, although scholars believe abundant footnotes are a sign of academic virtue, most readers find them a distraction. In this study, footnotes have been used sparingly; I have not, for example, footnoted references to the Carpenters' Minute Books (presently housed in the Carpenters' Hall) or Halifax newspapers, but instead have indicated such sources in the text. Footnotes have been used to note more obscure archival sources and debts to other secondary works. I would be pleased to make an academic paper on this subject, including many more footnotes, available to anyone wishing to track down my sources. Second, when quoting ungrammatical sentences from original documents, I have replaced the original words with a corrected version in brackets, rather than following each error in the original with a sanctimonious 'sic'. Bracketed words or additions to words in this text ([ ]) denote corrections of grammatical or spelling mistakes in the original documents.

I am very grateful to the archivists at the Public Archives of Nova Scotia and the Public Archives of Canada for all their help. Lewis Jackson, who poked through the records at the Public Archives in Ottawa and uncovered some wonderful gems, and Peter Lambly, who prepared a draft of the discussion of the economic aspects of construction after 1926, have my heartfelt thanks. I would also like to acknowledge the contribution of Gary Burrill, who has edited this book on behalf of Holdfast Press. I alone am responsible for the errors which remain. There are many people who have had to put up with the voracious demands this project has made—my long-suffering colleagues at *New Maritimes* and my equally long-suffering family, but by way of apology for my long months of seclusion, I dedicate it to my parents, John and Margaret McKay.

1

None But Skilled Workmen
1885-1900

In the present age, the rapid concentration of wealth in the hands of the few, gives them power to control the means of labor and dictate to the workers what they shall receive for the labor they perform. Every branch of labor is being rapidly monopolized, until the vast industrial interests of the world are now almost enslaved to the wealthy and privileged classes, and just in proportion as this state of affairs continues, the power of the capitalist increases and the working people are impoverished and subjected.

Look at the position occupied by the Carpenters and Joiners today. Our wages are lower than those of other trades who require less skill and furnish fewer tools. Year by year our vocation has lost the proud position it once occupied. It therefore becomes our duty to ask ourselves, shall we willingly permit our craft to sink lower and lower in the social scale until we are completely enslaved? Are we, who have done so much to build the world's wealth, not entitled to a just equivalent for what we do? Must we be forever without sufficient means to maintain ourselves and families in comfort and independence, to educate our children, and qualify them for the duties of life? Shall we be forced by division among ourselves to bow the suppliant knee to capital, and allow our craft to become the prey of the unscrupulous and designing[?]

> — Preamble of the Constitution of the Brotherhood of Carpenters and Joiners of America, 1881.

On 21 January 1884 a large audience packed the Halifax Lyceum and waited patiently for the speaker. The Lieutenant-Governor had graciously agreed to chair the meeting, and a number of prominent citizens occupied seats on the stage. It was a typical scene from Victorian Halifax, whose citizens frequently filled their winter months with lectures from missionaries and plays from wandering troupes of actors. But this lecture was very different from the standard fare offered Victorian lecture audiences.

The audience, to begin with, was unusual. Although the socially prominent dominated the platform, elsewhere in the hall workingmen made up the audience. Such a large gathering of workingmen for a lecture was unprecedented in the Halifax of the 1880s. The body which had called the meeting, the Amalgamated Trades Union (called the ATU or sometimes the AMTU), a labour group founded in 1881, was a novelty as well, the city's first large trade-union organization.

Once the lecturer finally arrived—he had been held up in Saint John and compelled to take a slow train—he showed himself to be out of the ordinary as well.

P.J. McGuire, the American who, along with Gustav Luebkert, had founded the Brotherhood of Carpenters and Joiners in 1881, wrote the ringing defence of the carpenters' craft which opens this chapter. McGuire had spent the last decade in labour organization and left-wing politics, in such groups as the Social Democratic Party of North America, the Greenback Labor Party, and the Knights of Labor. After the founding of the union, he threw himself into organizing activities; in one month in 1883 he toured 33 cities, selling trade unionism and socialism at every stop. He impressed thousands with his speeches on behalf of labour. He even impressed the stuffy Halifax newspapers. "He is a gentleman very intelligent of countenance and considerable presence, has a clear and distinct style of delivery, coupled with no small oratorical ability, and his lecture, which was delivered largely without manuscript, showed a comprehensive study and grasp of his subject," observed the Halifax *Morning Chronicle* in a review of his lecture.[1]

McGuire's Brotherhood had fixed its sights on Canada from its earliest days. Even at its first annual convention in 1881, the Brotherhood resolved "to enter into relations with the carpenters of Canada, with a view to bring them within our fold." The first Canadian locals were formed in Hamilton, Guelph, Toronto and Victoria.[2] McGuire's visit to Halifax was part of this expansion of the Brotherhood's activities.

His lecture, the first direct exposure a Halifax audience had to modern socialist thought, was an absorbing, soaring survey of the history of labour from Julius Caesar to the Knights of Labor. Spread over three nights, McGuire's talks aroused immense enthusiasm in the city.

The first part of his presentation was called "The Working Classes, their History and Struggles." McGuire took his audience through the pre-Christian era, when workers had been kept in a condition of slavery; only after centuries, he said, did the shackles fall from the workers' limbs and the "idea gained ground that there was as much dignity in labor as in those who are masters of labor." The stages of emancipation from serfdom were thoroughly traced, "till [today] the working class are wage workers, under liberty to work, true for often less remuneration than is earned, but only less, said the lecturer, when the working class itself is so stupid it does not organize to command more." A man digging a drain in the street was, from many points of view, to be more respected than the man who rolled luxuriously past in his carriage. "A great wrong was that workingmen should have to struggle from hand to mouth for their living, with their children nearly starving, and only to go to work as soon as they were able in competition with their parents." The history of the struggles for labour's emancipation was grand, and "it was the duty of the workingmen of to-day to keep up their claim to the history and make the line more glorious in the future." Concluding the first part of his presentation, McGuire said that "he might have said something in his remarks to shock some, but it was a good way to set people thinking, when they got in a certain rut, to shock them; after a while they would wake up and begin to inquire what struck them."

An equally large audience turned out for McGuire's second lecture, on "Trade Unionism and the Labor Question." McGuire took his text from the example of England. "Trade unionism had made it possible for men to face their employers, standing erect and comparatively independent. In the olden time the man who had a grievance about his pay approached his master with bated breath, and was fortunate if he was not discharged the moment he opened his mouth. It was vastly different now when by organization common cause was made, and each man stood by his brother."

Then McGuire turned to more practical questions. He spoke of the tendency of low wages to diminish skill: "As water seeks its own level," he argued, "the good workman must sink to the level of the botches.... Cheap labor produced cheap work—bad work buildings botched by scab bosses." Without unions, McGuire argued, building workers were reduced to cut-throat competition. "Two men meet on a building. They look askance at each other. One thinks the other wants to do more work than him, and thus get more pay. The result is a fatal competition which ends in both men doing more than a reasonable amount of labor, and thus shortening their job. It was a cut-throat business all through."

McGuire had a few good punches to throw at the employers in the audience. "Halifax was not likely to be invaded by any alarming influx of foreign labor. Wages were small enough here, God knows. The danger was that instead of people coming, those who were here would go away. The capitalists should look to it that their workmen should be kept at home and their houses tenanted."

McGuire ended his presentation by telling his audience that he would speak before the Amalgamated Trades Union and give them instructions as to organization. A vote of thanks was moved by two of Nova Scotia's foremost labour leaders, Robert Drummond, the leader of the Provincial Workmen's Association, the miners' union, and J.A. Mackasey, the leader of the Halifax longshoremen.

McGuire's third talk, which was not fully reported in the Halifax papers, concerned (according to the February, 1884 issue of *The Carpenter*, the organ of the Brotherhood) "the practical work of trades unions, and especially of the Carpenters Union of Halifax, which will result in that union joining the Brotherhood."

The most remarkable aspect of McGuire's visit to Halifax was the inspiration it appears to have given the Halifax working-class movement. That was the reason, in fact, why he had been invited. The Amalgamated Trades Union wanted (we read in *The Carpenter* of November 1883) "to hold a course of public lectures this winter on the Labour Question, and through this we hope to convert the great mass of men outside trade unions." The ATU's idea seems to have worked. For example, McGuire in his address had paid special attention to the boycott as a weapon in labour's struggle. After his visit to Halifax, the city's workers adopted the strategy wholeheartedly. "The boycotting movement is taking good hold here as a result of the teachings of P.J. McGuire, and was first introduced by him during his visit here last winter" noted the Halifax correspondent of *The Carpenter* in October, 1884. Boycotts had commenced against the *Daily Herald* and Moirs bakery. As for McGuire's own craft, the local carpenters' union was expanding, according to the same correspondent, at a rate of 3 or 4 members each meeting and was launching a struggle for an 11% raise.

McGuire appears to have given local workingmen confidence in themselves, for 1884, with its strikes, boycotts, and political campaigns, was the most dramatic year the Halifax working-class movement had ever seen.

Of course, one man, even a P.J. McGuire, does not a movement make. The Halifax working-class movement, born in the 1860s and nearly wiped out by the recession of the 1870s, had revived in 1881. As for McGuire's own craft, the Halifax carpenters and joiners could claim a long history of organization and struggle by the time of his visit.

As early as 1857, the journeymen carpenters had made collective demands upon their employers. In the *Morning Journal and Commerical Advertizer* they argued that if they did not receive higher wages, "it will be the means of driving from this Province smart and intelligent men to improve their condition in the neighboring Republic." Seven years later, the House Joiners' Union Society of Halifax (founded in 1863 and incorporated in 1864), backed up a similar call for higher wages by going on strike. Like most unions during the depressed 1870s, this carpenters' union collapsed.

It was revived in 1881, the same year that the Brotherhood of Carpenters and Joiners was born in the United States. On 3 June, 1881, at a meeting held at the Agricultural Hall, the carpenters formed the House Joiners' Union of Halifax, for the purpose, according to the *Acadian Recorder*, "of protecting their trade, and demanding a general increase of wages." The new union was quickly successful. The *Halifax Chronicle* suggested that by 24 March 1883, of the city's 350 carpenters, only 75 were not in the union. *The Carpenter* took its first notice of the Halifax carpenters in April 1883, when it commented favourably on the activities of the "House Joiners' Association of Halifax and Dartmouth." By November 1883, the Halifax correspondent was writing: "Everything has been done to get our Union to join the Brotherhood, but owing to the lack of interest in our local union we resolved that as soon as a hundred names could be secured who would pledge themselves to stand by the Brotherhood, we should then apply for a charter. This number is nearly on our list...." *The Carpenter*, the correspondent added, was received in the city's Trades Union Hall.

From the *Acadian Recorder* we may glean an impression of the issues which agitated this forerunner to Local 83: low wages, the high cost of housing, the continuing flow of craftsmen to the United States. "One of the largest and most enthusiastic trades' meetings ever held in the city of Halifax took place on Monday evening, March 6, in Hesslein's Building, the occasion being a regular monthly meeting of the House Carpenters' and Joiners' Association of Halifax and Dartmouth.... After the regular business had been disposed of, and several new members initiated, one of the members [most likely John Saxton, the chief leader of the carpenters and later recording secretary of the Amalgamated Trades Union] was called to the floor, and with spirit and energy delivered an address on the progress of the organization and the state of the trade in general; the speaker called the attention of the meeting to the high rate of taxation and the rate of living at present in Halifax, and the low rate of wages the joiners were receiving from their employers to meet so extortionate a demand. He also referred to the general increase of wages throughout the Upper Provinces, also to the great field for immigration to the Northwest Territory and the United States and finally concluded that unless the employers of the City of Halifax would further the interest of their journeymen in connection with the above trade, they would have to leave their native province and seek a home on foreign soil. He also trusted that another month would swell the ranks of the organization with the presence of every carpenter and joiner in Halifax and Dartmouth."

Halifax had not slept through the labour storms shaking the continent in the 1880s. Echoes of the turbulent struggle between the craft unions and the Knights of Labor could be heard in the city. One issue raised by this struggle was the proper way to organize workingmen. The Knights were willing to organize both the skilled and the unskilled; craft unions concentrated mainly on the skilled. Although the Knights were never important in Halifax, the city's major labour organization, the Amalgamated Trades Union, shared many of their ideas about organizing. The ATU saw its role as broadly educational, it emphasized political action, and it sought to merge the activities of local craft unions.

In the 1880s the ATU was just as important a voice for the carpenters as was Local 83. The distinctions between the two organizations were often blurred. For example, when P.J. McGuire, one of the principal architects of the craft-oriented American Frederation of Labour (AFL), visited Halifax, he spoke glowingly of the work of the Knights of Labor and supported the ATU. Only gradually did the craft unionists and the ATU advocates come to see the tasks of organization in quite different ways.

For John Saxton, the major organizer among the Halifax carpenters in their days before affiliation with the Brotherhood, or Michael Walsh, the ambitious politico who first surfaced in the House Joiners' Society of the 1860s, the Amalgamated Trades Union, not the individual craft unions, was the most important arena. In the ATU's headquarters, Mechanics' Hall ("mechanic" was a word commonly used in the nineteenth century for "artisan") on Barrington Street, four amalgamated societies—the painters, carpenters, bricklayers and bakers—conducted their affairs jointly. The ATU's horizons were limited to the skilled mechanics, and it aimed at what compositor James Fultz called "the mutual improvement to be derived from the formation of a union where the mechanics might be better acquainted with their fellows and aim to elevate and educate their class." Four members from each union were elected and formed a convention for the selection of officers to the ATU. Although similar in some respects to a labour council, the ATU actually seems to have been not so much a council "representing" the individual unions, as a single body with its member unions functioning more like sub-committees. (Rank-and-file workers and not just representatives were expected to attend meetings of the ATU.) This was what was meant by the "amalgamation of the various Trade Unions" spoken of in the press, and the main reason why the ATU took such a direct role in pushing workers' campaigns. The ATU entailed a degree of merger and unity among skilled workers that Halifax would not see again until 1919.

It was the ATU, and not Local 83, which first pressed for protection for carpenters and other building workers in the local labour market and on the new City Hall project. As reported by the *Chronicle* on 29 March 1883, the ATU called upon the city to impose a tax on outside builders and others who came to work in Halifax without paying anything into the city coffers. The ATU would also, very controversially, take the lead in pushing issues related to the building trades in 1886 and 1887, while in this later year Local 83 was reported in the July issue of *The Carpenter* to be "prostrate."

The House Joiners' Union was successful in raising wages from 90¢ per day in 1882 to between $1.40 and $1.65 per day, according to *The Carpenter* in February 1884. In June it was reported to be struggling for an 11% wage increase, and the correspondent tied the chances of the local union's affiliating with the Brotherhood closely to the outcome of the agitation. "If the carpenters receive the advance, there will be no trouble in joining the Brotherhood under their constitution," he wrote, "but the city is crowded with scabs and botches and many of our old members are returning to the ranks, because they begin to see that organization is the only weapon against low wages. In some cases the bosses here don't own as much as would purchase a half-pound of shingle nails." By September, the correspondent noted that the membership of the union was growing, but that it was hesitant about seeking affiliation with the International: "Our carpenter[s'] union is growing steadily, but as we are on a low dues basis and our wages are low, there seems to be some drawback to joining the Brotherhood. Nevertheless the spirit is now more favourable and all we want is a full attendance to pass upon the question. Since we organized wages have gone up to $1.75 a day—a gain of 35 cents per day through unionism. The idea of labour organization is taking strong hold here, we have a central body called the Amalgamated Union of Halifax and [P.J. McGuire's] visit has kept us busy starting new societies."

So even before the affiliation of Local 83 to the United Brotherhood on 3 February 1885, Halifax carpenters felt themselves to be organized in the broad North American labour movement. When *The Carpenter* surveyed the progress the Brotherhood had made in May, 1884, it was technically in error when it claimed that "Now we stretch as a union from Halifax to San Francisco," but it was broadly correct in seeing the Halifax carpenters as an organized union in harmony (but not yet affiliated) with the international body.

It is difficult to say why the local union waited until January, 1885, to affiliate with the Brotherhood. Possibly carpenters worried about the need to pay more money, and the requirement that the local union include 100 members may also have deterred it. (It had nowhere near this number in 1885 when finally it did join.) Possibly the carpenters were divided between those who still saw their role as being in the ATU first and the local society second, and those who saw their allegiance to the international craft as coming before their affiliation with the ATU. It is striking that the old carpenter activists who had linked themselves firmly to the ATU had only minor roles in this new organization. The affiliation of Local 83 may well have originated in the storms of dissatisfaction which overtook the ATU in 1884 when it ran into financial difficulties. Although the bitter struggles in other cities between the strategies of the Knights and the American Federation of Labor were not replicated in Halifax, there is at least some evidence suggesting that the strained relations between the ATU and Local 83 were rooted in the same fundamental questions of trade union organization.

The high point of the disagreement between the two organizations came when the ATU took up the cause of building workers on the new City Hall being undertaken by the Amherst contractors Rhodes, Curry & Co. (This was probably the first independent action taken by a labour centre in Halifax politics.) The ATU wrote to Rhodes, Curry in 1888 stating that it would not allow any union man to go to work on the building until he had received his back pay from a former contractor on the project. However, at a meeting on 23 April, the union denounced those who had written over its signature to criticize the role of the mayor in the building project. It was "Resolved, That as the Mayor had promised the Amalgamated Trades Union deputation not to sign the City Hall contract until the deputation had arranged, either to have a clause inserted compelling the contractors to employ city labor, or to call a mass meeting of Halifax ratepayers; and as the committee did not report until to-night, no member of this union had the information and authority to write in opposition to His Worship...." This makes it clear not only that the ATU believed itself to have the right to intervene directly in a case of this sort, but that it was becoming embroiled in partisan politics.

The eclipse of the ATU and the rise of Local 83 went hand in hand, and relations between the two bodies were not cordial. Local 83 severed its connection with the ATU early in 1888. According to the Local's minutes, representatives of the ATU asked for the carpenters' assistance in forming a labour council on 5 February 1889 and "some of them expressed the wish to have Local 83 again amalgamated with them"; the question was considered by a committee, and on 27 February 1889 the union decided that "while this union is in favour of a labor council of the building Trades they will not enter the A.M.T.U." A split had occurred in the Halifax labour movement between the ATU activists and certain of the craft unions.

The dramatic visit of McGuire to Halifax in 1884 brought a new force to local activists. He brought local struggles over wages and hours into a context which spanned the continents and centuries. Local 83's birth date, then, might be put in 1881, when its local forerunner was organized, or 1885, with its affiliation to the international union, or in 1888, when it declared its independence from the ATU. But perhaps the most persuasive date to pick would be 1884, when P.J. McGuire mounted the platform of the Lyceum and, for the first time, explained to Halifax craftsmen that they must fight the employers as a class.

But what moved Halifax craftsmen to adopt craft unionism in the first place? And why did they bring these unions into much larger international bodies? To understand the deeper roots of Local 83, we have to look at the ways the carpenters' view of themselves was being changed as the nineteenth century progressed.

In the early nineteenth century the craft of the carpenter required a wide-ranging proficiency in most forms of woodwork. It was carried out in small workshops and on building sites, under the supervision of a master carpenter, generally a man who had risen from the ranks of the journeymen. The master craftsman did not himself initiate building projects, nor did he employ craftsmen other than carpenters. The building crafts were very much separate entities, working together on specific job sites, but only as masters in each craft contracted to do parts of the work on a particular project.

In early nineteenth-century Halifax, journeymen and masters collaborated in maintaining a strong sense of the craft. In 1798, the Carpenters, Joiners and Cabinet-makers' Society bound masters and journeymen together for benevolent purposes. By 1821, this Society (or its successor) owned the Carpenters' Hall on Salter Street.

Some documents from the very early organizations of carpenters and joiners still survive. According to the 1833 *Rules* of the Brother Carpenters' Society, apparently a lineal descendant of the eighteenth-century body, "Persons eligible to join this Society, must be Carpenters, Joiners, Cabinet Makers, and Turners in wood, between twenty-one and thirty-five years of age, of good character, and free from any defect." There were strict rules governing the spending of the Society's money for the relief of its members: "No money to be paid out of the funds of the Society, until they amount to Fifty Pounds currency—No Member shall be entitled to any relief from the Society until he has been one year a member thereof, nor if he be four quarters in arrears, then if he is confined to his bed, he shall receive Ten Shillings weekly; if not confined to his house, though unable to work, seven shillings and six pence." Only if a unanimous vote were taken would "Any member claiming relief, whose sickness or poverty is the effect of his own imprudence," obtain relief from the organization. Upon the death of a member, the sum of forty shillings was to be spent on his burial, and three pounds annually were to be given to the widow, "so long as she remains in a state of virtuous widowhood." Members of the Society were instructed, on pain of financial penalty, to attend the funeral of a Brother Carpenter, "to meet at the Hall, with their aprons, and follow the corpse to the grave, in a regular orderly manner—the Officers of the Society wearing their official emblems, taking the lead."

In 1850, a Carpenters' Society of Halifax was incorporated.[3] We find the Carpenters' Society performing such deeds as donating gifts to the Catholic orphanage, giving sumptuous dinners, and carrying out the benevolent functions of visiting and supporting sick members. Evidently having passed into oblivion in the 1860s, the Society had been an appropriate organization for helping the journeymen and master carpenters of a traditional craft, in which both employer and employee alike considered themselves skilled "mechanics."

By the 1860s, however, the organization of the industry had changed. Increased size, the emergence of "builders" who integrated diverse crafts under one roof and could contract for whole projects, a large expansion of the industry in the wake of a major fire in the centre of the city—all these tended to break down the old unity of the craft.[4] Yet even as we watch journeymen and masters, capital and labour, slowly draw apart, we still hear the language of the old craft. When the house and ship joiners petitioned their employers in 1857, they noted, "We feel confident that you will aid and assist us by your sanction to elevate and place the industrious mechanic, who earns his bread by the sweat of his brow, in a position respectable to himself, his employer, and the community at large." And when the House Joiners' Union was born in 1863-64, master carpenters were prominent among the leading members of the new trade union. The rituals and symbols of the union were classic models of craft pride. In 1864, the first House Joiners' Union commissioned a handsome silk banner, made in London at the staggering cost of $250, one side of which depicted a carpenter's outfit of tools, and the other a portrait of trees being felled in a forest. Across the banner was written, in Latin, "By diligence and perserverance we overcome all things."

Many masters would have graduated from the ranks of the journeymen; many journeymen could realistically aspire to be masters. From their point of view, what counted was "the trade" as a whole. But just the fact that a separate journeymen's organization existed meant that "the trade" was now splitting into two distinct camps. And after the long crisis of the 1870s these camps surfaced in the city once again.

The decade of the 1880s was transitional: the features of a new organization of the craft were discernible but not yet dominant. The world of the craftsmen was slowly being undermined, especially by three important and related economic changes.

The first was the mechanization of significant parts of woodworking and construction. Production was standardized in new ways. Sashes, doors, and mouldings were now frequently produced in factories. More than most building craftsmen, carpenters faced directly the challenges of technological change.

The craft of carpentry tended to be broken down into its component parts. The contrast was increasingly drawn between the old-time *joiner,* who could do all types of work in a building (from planning the project to rough carpentry in the foundations, to finish work calling for the skills of a cabinetmaker), and the *general carpenter,* limited to rough construction work and the fixing in place of materials prepared elsewhere.

"There was a time we cut out the doors and the sash and the wooden trim that goes around the wash-board and base in a room—all the woodwork in the construction of a building was prepared by hand or motor power machinery," remarked P.J. McGuire in 1899. But now, he said, the use of steam-power machinery had shifted production of doors, sash, and wood-trim to the northwest United States, where children were employed at tender years. On some planing machines, he continued, productivity was fourteen times greater than by hand; the enhanced productivity achieved by moulding machinery was almost as great. Tiling, grooving and flooring, "all the manifold branches of woodwork," were now affected, McGuire said, by mechanization. In places like New York, carpenters on the best buildings could go in and case around the doors, hang the doors, put in the sash and the inside blinds; but other work tended to be now either of other materials (such as stone, terra cotta, tiling, or metal of some kind) or prepared in factories. Carpenters could no longer rely on board, sash and trim work for employment during the unfavourable winter months, as they had in the past.[5]

Nova Scotia, with excellent lumber supplies and a quickly developing industrial economy, was not backward in following this international trend. In mid-nineteenth-century Halifax, the Acadia Moulding Factory employed the latest patented machinery (planers with tongue-and-groove apparatus, large lathes, sash moulding machinery) to transform lumber from Sheet Harbour, Saint John, and Charleston into "doors, door frames, sashes, mouldings, etc." Not only were the proprietors willing to supply mechanics with the latest in wood work, but they themselves offered to contract for the erection of houses.

When an admiring reporter visited James Dempster's mill just north of the Halifax Commons in 1880, he noted the heavy machinery for planing purposes, where the lumber was prepared from the rough and made suitable for the various uses to which it was put, as well as the standard moulding devices; he also noted "a sand-paperer, which we believe is the only one of its kind in these parts, and which must certainly be a great saving in labor, as one man, with the aid of it, can do a half a dozen men's work, and at the same time, do it more thoroughly." Dempster gave work to 25 men working full time, and boasted of new markets in Bermuda. By 1888, Dempster told a Royal Commission investigating the relations between capital and labour that he had between 40 and 50 hands on the average. He noted that about 75% of these men were "skilled mechanics"; but added that "each one may have skill for the work he is doing." About 13 or 14 of his employees worked on the machines; about 20 of his men were "joiners and finishers," and the remainder "do different sorts of work. Some of them run a circular saw. Some of them get in stock and put it into the drying room or get it out and lower it down, and so on." Dempster was making the same point that McGuire was later to make: the new machinery tended to break down the carpenters' traditionally rounded skills.

Secondly, general contractors — men who tendered for contracts, maintained a force of craftsmen of various sorts at the disposal of the companies, and deployed this force on large projects — became far more important after 1880. Such general contracting flourished in a buoyant market for private housing and institutional building. The employer was now not always a "master craftsman"; he might well be a businessman, with a wide range of investments. A journeyman could scarcely consider a builder like S.M. Brookfield, with interests ranging from the Halifax Graving Dock to the cotton factory, to be a "brother mechanic" with exactly the same interests as himself. Brookfield's father came to Halifax from New Brunswick to take a contract with the imperial government for the construction of Fort Clarence on the Dartmouth side of the harbour. The Brookfields won most of the imperial building contracts in Halifax and constructed many of the city's largest buildings. They owned a planing mill off Inglis Street and a palatial residence, considered one of the finest in the province, on Pleasant. In 1888, the same Royal Commission on Capital and Labour was informed by Brookfield that he employed an average number of 100 journeymen during the year, paying "bench hands" who worked inside $1.75 per day, stone cutters $2.50, and labourers from $1.00 to $1.25. He not only employed many different kinds of craftsmen, but was able to combine ship work with land work profitably.

S.M. Brookfield was a prime Halifax example of the general contractor of the 1880s. There were many others. John McInnis, of the firm McIntosh and McInnis, when questioned by the same Royal Commission, referred to his firm as "general contractors and lumber dealers." He reported that on the average it employed about 40 men, although in busy times this figure could rise to 100 and in slack times drop to 20. He said of his workmen that some of his hands did "not profess to be good mechanics," and these were paid from $1.25 to $1.50, in contrast to the first-class journeymen's rate of $1.60. In contrast with Dempster, he employed no machine hands.

When McGuire told the Halifax craftsmen about the impact of new machines and methods, they could make a connection with their own experience. Many of them now worked in ill-ventilated and unsanitary shops ringing with the sounds of the new machinery. Journeyman Michael McNeil, for example, testified in 1888 that the air in his shop was filled with dust from "sandpapers"; asked if there was enough dust to be injurious to the men, he replied, "Well, I do not know—I cannot really tell, it does not seem to hurt me or any of our crowd."

Thirdly, the growth of general contracting contributed to a new sense that journeymen had distinct interests to defend within the construction industry. The artisanal language of "brother mechanics" slowly waned and was replaced with a more combative trade unionism. The emergence of stable trade union structures in all the major building trades of the 1880s, and the affiliation of these unions with international organizations based in the United States, suggested that the division between journeymen and large masters was widening.

The emergence of trade unionism did not change craft attitudes overnight. The old customs and usages of building trades workers were defended by workers throughout the 1880s and 1890s. Eight stonemasons and bricklayers went on strike against S.M. Brookfield at the site of the new Halifax cotton factory in 1883 because of Brookfield's tampering with their right to the traditional water-break. (Brookfield had fired the water-boy for allegedly mixing liquor with the water.) In the case of the carpenters, some small masters formerly had been prominent trade unionists; one firm cordially gave the union a gift subscription to a trade journal.

And most small masters and journeymen agreed on one thing: rural migrants were ruining the Halifax crafts by driving down wages and lowering standards. Over and over, before the Royal Commission on the Relations of Capital and Labour in 1888, they returned to this problem.

Michael McNeil complained, "Some of these fellows away out in the country come in here and terribly affect us.... Some come in during the bulding season, stay 4 or 5 months and go out home again.... I do not consider them carpenters, but all the same they come in in place of a mechanic when they come here." Asked about the rates demanded by such rural craftsmen, McNeil exclaimed: "...they go to work for almost nothing."

P.F. Martin, the leader of the painters, echoed McNeil's complaint. "Every Tom, Dick and Harry come into this town from all parts of the

Dominion that know nothing of painting whatever and call themselves painters and they work for less wages and deprive skilled mechanics of work," he reported. George Tanner, another painter, told the Commissioners that "There is a vast amount of unskilled labor comes in here. A man comes in here and calls himself a painter and he is not fit for anything unless it is on outside work and then when the busy time comes in he works for less wages and this is an injustice to us."

Arthur C. Lessell, Local 83's most important nineteenth-century leader, was equally emphatic in seeing the rural craftsmen as a grave threat to Halifax trade unions. "We suffer here most terribly from unskilled labor, especially during the busy season; this unskilled labor has now crept in and destroyed the trade. There are skilled hands now in this town working 25 or 30 years, but according as they die out very few men are coming in to fill their places; I am now, of course, speaking of men able to take a specification and plan and carry it out themselves." In the summer season, he went on, "any quantity of unskilled labor comes into the town and usurps the place of mechanics. It is a well known fact that in our trade the most money is in the rough work, and if you get unskilled labor to do the rough work it is better for the employer."

And who, the Commissioners asked, were these men who were so undermining the Halifax carpenters? Were they farm workers? Lessell replied, "There are some on farms and others do fishing, and they come around with an axe on their shoulder and offer to put on shingles and do other outdoor work; then in winter they go back to their homes as they have saved enough during the summer to keep them, and they pay no taxes here. They save all the proceeds of their work and live on almost nothing." Many, Lessell noted, came from Chezzetcook on the Eastern Shore. If only the union could enforce indentured apprenticeship, shorter hours, and higher pay — these reforms "would have a tendency to use up all the surplus labor, and then create demand, our surplus labor here is not so great, and naturally wages would go up...."

But until then, what could Lessell and Local 83 do? A cardinal principle, indeed *the* cardinal principle, of building craft unionism was preventing entry to the crafts by workers thought to be less skilled—like these countrymen and out-of-work fishermen who were so disdainfully dismissed as "botches." They were thought to be beneath the abilities needed for craft unionists. One answer, Lessell thought (he was at heart a very old-fashioned and traditional craftsman) was to talk to the master carpenters. If only they could see the harm this fatal competition in the labour market was inflicting on everyone! If only they would bring back indentured, legally enforceable apprenticeship to safeguard skill within the craft!

"I contend that the organization of labor is a benefit to the employer in every sense of the word," Lessell eloquently proclaimed in 1888. "I think if the provisions of the labor organization alone were carried out and the constitution adhered to, the employers would find that they had the better workmen in their employ. It induces sobriety as one of its main provisions, and I have known instances of men who have been habitual drunkards who, by its means, have been reformed. That is one thing that is a gain to any community.... We are indeed very particular as to the men we take in. We desire to take none but skilled workmen, but in a community like this we cannot get all skilled men, yet we do the best we can."

His was the classic outlook of excluding those men who, for whatever reason, did not measure up to the ideal of the craft. Local 83 was not supposed to admit any man not capable of earning the average wage, (although this wage in Halifax was a small one, and there were few employees who did not earn it). Desirous of admitting only first-class mechanics, Lessell admitted that Local 83 had to take others besides. With the craft swamped in the building season by rural migrants and menaced by the increased impact of machines, appeals to the employers to enforce essential union discipline were apt to be ineffective, for the simple reason that the employer was under as much competitive pressure as his men. Admitting machine men to the union—something Local 83 was reluctant to do in the nineteenth-century—meant changing the whole basis of the craft. And so the union tended to see its main task as excluding the unskilled and the rural craftsmen, and this gave many of its policies and statements the same tone as that used by the "labour aristocracy" in Britain—a tone of high respectability and bitter contempt for the unorganized and rural.[6] The difference between Halifax and Britain, however, was that the local craftsmen were, to a far greater degree, on the defensive.

The defence of the craft often took the form of trying to shore up the apprenticeship system, in decline since the mid-nineteenth century. Control over the number and training of apprentices in the building trades was a fiercely contested issue in this decade. Painters were in the forefront of the battle. In 1884, the informal quota of three apprentices per shop was broken, and the union settled for an unusual written agreement, which was, however, later violated. Painters in 1888 complained bitterly of the attacks on apprenticeship customs. William Johnston, a house painter, told the Royal Commission, "There are too many apprentices in a shop. We have known two men to be in a shop and nine apprentices, and good mechanics, with families, walking about in fine weather, and when the men are discharged the boys are kept on—that is of course for the rough work." The unwritten principle of apprenticeship was that the boys were supposed to acquire a general experience of the craft so that they would, on completion, be full-fledged journeymen. But in painting, the apprentices were kept on the rough work and priming about the shop. Apprentices, far from being used to bolster the craft, were simply a reserve army of cheap labour the employers could call upon at will. "Now and then they have work for them," Johnston remarked, "but when the work is slack the apprentices are discharged, and they have to stay idle until spring opens again, and it is the same all around and that is where the main trouble is; a boy only serves a few months out of the year and by the time he becomes a man why he cannot claim the wages he should."

The problem was just as serious in carpentry. While some firms still observed the traditional five-year apprenticeship, many shops simply avoided hiring apprentices. President Arthur Lessell argued in 1888 that without formal, indentured apprentices, the quality of work was slipping. A boy quickly picked up a smattering of knowledge, he claimed, "and then he thinks he knows the business, and he hires himself out as a journeyman; of course some parts of the work he can do, others he cannot do so well, and when he comes down to technical parts he cannot do anything at all...." Without indentured apprentices, the carpenters "able to take a specification and plan and carry it out themselves" were being replaced by unskilled botches from Chezzetcook who dragged down the standards of the craft.

"None but skilled workmen": it was a classic motto for nineteenth-century craftsmen. For men like Lessell, who dominated the union from its birth to the mid-1890s, it had the unquestioned ring of truth. But there were forces at work which would make this outlook an embattled one indeed in the closing years of the nineteenth century.

Our view of the world of the Halifax carpenter in the 1890s is much more complete than the glimpses we are afforded from the 1880s, and we are able to evaluate the day-to-day life of the union in the latter decade, as workingmen responded to these new challenges to the craft. The evidence suggests a craft facing many battles, but able to hold its own on the contested terrain of the Halifax construction industry.

The majority of Halifax carpenters still worked for the traditional craft shops or for the local, securely based general contractors. The union's base lay in such large firms as Brookfield's and Mackintosh and McInnis, and in a dozen or so small, four- or five-man shops. In 1889, as the Minutes of 29 May reveal, Local 83 was organized in 13 shops, a majority of those employing carpenters. Later in 1889, it had also spread to the Intercolonial Railway Car Works, the employees of the Imperial Government, the Dock Yard, and the Drydock.

Local 83 was not, of course, a large and powerful institution within the

city, and most citizens of Halifax remained blissfully unaware of its existence. But its importance to its members and the Brotherhood as a whole
should not be underestimated. Local 83 was a standard-bearer for international craft unionism in the region. It was in correspondence with carpenters' unions in Yarmouth, Cape Breton, and Amherst. It supported
Halifax printers in their long struggles against the *Herald* and *Mail* in the
1890s and sent $25 off to support striking Halifax weavers. In contrast
to the murky struggles with the ATU in the 1880s and the incessant
jurisdictional battles among AFL unions in the twentieth century, there
were almost no jurisdictional conflicts in the period 1890-1926, with the
important exception that members of the Shipwrights' and Caulkers'
Union, an organization as old as that of the carpenters, were refused
admission to Local 83 unless they withdrew from their own old and
withering organization.

In the early 1890s Local 83 was a significant element of the international
Brotherhood as well. Its President, Arthur C. Lessell, was asked to
become an international organizer in 1889 and was one of three Canadian
district organizers listed in the Convention Proceedings of 1892. (The
other two lived in Toronto and Winnipeg.)[7]

Relations with the Brotherhood were generally amicable, but there was
some friction in balancing Canadian and American standards. There is
solid evidence that Local 83 wanted greater local autonomy on such
nuts-and-bolts questions as dues and benefits. The Local felt that international policies regarding protective funds and head taxes should take into
account the lower wage rates in Canada. One reason it felt this way was
that it did not have a large financial base. On 5 May, 1891, the union's
funds totalled $224.07, and it had to meet monthly expenses of $62.59.
Some officers were paid: the recording secretary, for example, was voted a
salary of $20 in 1888. There was not much to draw on when P.J. McGuire,
intent as ever on centralizing the union's treasury, pestered the Local for
money. (There was even less after the financial secretary resigned on 20
February 1894 when an auditor's report revealed a deficit in his accounts.)

In September, 1890, the Local moved that "the local unions should be
allowed to regulate their own dues," and also demanded that provisions in
the international union's new constitution, making proxy votes possible,
be extended to the Dominion. The question of dues led to Local 83's
decisive rejection of the new constitution on 29 September 1890, by a vote
of 156-0. By 22 November 1892, feelings in Halifax had grown so heated
on this question that the Local took the unusual step of corresponding
with all the carpenters' locals in the Dominion to "endeavour to get their
Co-Operation in Appealing to the G[eneral] B[oard] to Allow Said
Unions the Privilege of fixing their own rate of dues per Month."

For the average rank-and-file member this union was important not because it was a branch of the international Brotherhood, but because it performed three basic functions.

One was that it gave him a "passport" to better-paying jobs elsewhere, often in Massachusetts, where the union's locals were in frequent correspondence with Local 83 as to the standing of emigré carpenters. Obtaining this passport was perhaps the best form of unemployment insurance nineteenth-century craftsmen had.

The second basic function was the relief of the sick. Assistance to sick members had been a theme of the first Carpenters' Society, and it was a prominent activity now of Local 83. (One reason why masters kept their membership in the Local may well have been so that they would remain eligible for such relief.) "Sick committees" based on city wards visited ailing members and could give them assistance out of the Local's sick benefit fund. For many members, this was the principal reason for the union's existence. So important was the sick benefit fund that the president of Local 83 fell from office in 1897 over one particular sick benefit case. In the absence of the modern welfare state, it is easy to appreciate why members wanted the protection afforded by the fund; it is also clear that the granting of such local aid led to divisive questions about the worthiness of its recipients. The local sick benefit scheme was abolished on 9 May 1898 by a vote of 16-7.

The Brotherhood itself provided benefits to a member (provided he had not fallen into arrears for three months) of $300 in case of accident pertaining to the trade, $50 in the event of his wife's death, and $200 to the widow in a case of the member's death. Of 30¢ per month dues in the late 1880s, approximately 10¢ per month went towards such benefits.

The union's third important function was the attempt to regulate the conditions of the craft. Although migrant rural carpenters and the collapse of apprenticeship worried the union, it did have two strong cards left to play. It could insist on high standards for those who wished to join and receive benefits from the union, and it could impose a closed shop and a network of shop stewards on the best shops.

Applicants who wished admission to the union were examined closely. Some were excluded automatically. The wife of a carpenter applied on 16 July 1890 and was informed that no wives were allowed. This was not surprising: Local 83 on 6 January 1891 had given the twelve-months' hoist—that is, politely rejected—even the idea of votes for women, let alone their admission to the ranks.

Others, however, had to pass through the Local's rigorous screening procedure. When names were proposed for initiation, the Conductor retired with the candidates and asked them questions on the craft. Then the candidates were ballotted for, with members submitting white and black beans to register their opinions; if there were too many black beans, the prospective member was not admitted. (Even after a favourable vote of 36 white to 16 black beans, William Noseworthy, a candidate proposed at the meeting of 19 February 1895, was the subject of "considerable discussion" before the Local decided to admit him.) When eight men applied for admission on 20 August 1890, "Some discussion then took place as to the eligibility of some of the candidates to become members of this union[.] On motion it was decided to appoint an Investigating committee to enquire into the candidates' qualifications." William Walker, a candidate who applied on 2 September 1890, was denied admission because "of a doubt existing as to his qualifications to become a member of this union...." Even after Walker presented a note from a builder certifying that he had served a five-year apprenticeship, Local 83 refused to entertain his application without "more definite information." P.J. McGuire then intervened on Walker's behalf, but to no avail: he still was not admitted. Since the crucial criterion of eligibility was one's future ability to earn the standard rate—a qualification which rested on subjective estimates of a candidate's abilities as much as anything—the Local had a lot of power to deny entry to the city's best-paying carpentry jobs.

The question of the closed shop is a matter of some contention. The historian Richard Price notes a good deal of ambivalence among British rank-and-file trade unionists regarding non-unionists, not all of whom were regarded as enemies.[8] The same point applies to Halifax in the 1880s, but not in the 1890s. In the 1880s, the doctrine that trade unionists should not work with non-unionists was applied selectively. Asked by the Royal Commission if "the members of the union decline to work with non-union men?" carpenter James Brodie replied, "I think they do not, not as I know of. We always try to get them to join, but there is no objection to them." Alexander Northup, a prominent stalwart of Local 83, thought, on the other hand, that the by-laws expressly prohibited union men from working with non-union men. (Unfortunately, nobody on the Commission thought to ask President Lessell.) The intensity of the Local's feelings against the "scab" (a label attached not to all non-unionists, but to those who betrayed the best interests of the craft) was suggested by the report in *The Carpenter* of Local 83's presence in the first Halifax Labour Day parade, in 1888, when one of its members carried a model of a giant mallet, with the sign, "For Levelling Scabs." The minutes of 1889-1891 convey the same hostile sentiment: in one case the Union resolved to get rid of the "scab LaPierre" on 20 February 1889, and had succeeded in doing so by 5 March. Members were charged with working with non-unionists on 19 November 1890, and non-unionists were reported working at Johnston & Caldwell on 14 January 1891. Finally, on 15 April 1891, the minutes record that "A motion by bro Murphy that no union carpenter work with a non union carpenter after May 15th, also to be published in the public press, after some discussion passed."

The closed shop, however, fell outside the union's grasp in the closing years of the nineteenth century. The tide turned against the closed shop in the second half of 1893. M.E. Keefe, the prominent Halifax contractor, was threatened that year with a strike if he did not stop employing suspended members; there is no indication that he complied. One member was reported working with a non-unionist on Lawler's Island; non-unionists were reported at John McInnis & Sons; a man without a "genuine Clearance Card from Union 279 of Harvey Ill." was reported at work at S.M. Brookfield's; a committee of two waited upon James Dempster to request that he fire two non-unionists in his mill. This last case was a decisive indication that closed-shop policy was weakening. When the union sent a delegation to interview Dempster, "he expressed himself satisfied with his men Joining our Union but thought he had no right in forcing them." Dempster interviewed the non-unionist, discovered that "on no condition would he join Union 83," and the union threatened Dempster "that unless his Non Union men come to our terms that all Union men in his employ will be called out and all Union men at large will refuse to work and Stock from his Mill." The result, however, was the end of Local 83 in Dempster's mill. By 4 December 1894, Brother A.C. Collings was asking if something could not be done "to Compel non union men to Join our Union who are working along with Union men in Various firms especially where there is a Majority...." An interesting test of the union's attitudes towards non-unionists was the defeat on 7 August 1895 of a resolution that "each Member have the privilege of inviting any ex member or Outside Carpenter to labor day parade." Instead, the union demanded that "no outsiders or ex Members with the exception of those whose name[s] are on the Roll books since the beginning of the year 1895" be allowed to join the Labour Day Parade.

Yet it would be a mistake to think that the inability to maintain the closed shop spelled the end of the union's power. The union commanded a compelling loyalty among its followers. A total of 155 members turned out on average for meetings in 1889, a far higher turnout than is found today. In the small and intimate city that was Halifax in the 1880s and 1890s, the union carpenters were all well-known to each other (indeed, there were a good many father-and-son combinations in the union). The shame of "violating one's obligation" and losing face in the eyes of one's peers was probably as effective as any other deterrent to breaking union rules. Such traditions as visiting and raising money for sick and impoverished members, and of paying the dues of ailing brothers to keep them in benefit, must have bound men closely together. The member charged on

2 August 1892 with "conduct unbecoming a union man," or the brother censured from the chair on 17 September 1890 for "use of an impolite expression," faced the unwritten assumptions and code of honour which guided the Local's formal workplace rules.

The union's success in enforcing any of these rules depended on the shop stewards, whose role was far more critical in this period than at any other. (There were no "walking delegates" or "business agents" in the Local.) Shop stewards performed such duties as taking up collections for injured brothers, enforcing the closed shop, and reporting on conditions in each workplace. When rural craftsmen ("hatchet and saw men" they were called) were reported working at the Drydock, the shop steward there was harshly reprimanded for not doing his duty and it was resolved that all shop stewards were to report monthly. When the union was strong, the shop stewards submitted regular reports on each workplace. In 1889, for example, William Carroll, shop steward in S.M. Brookfield's employ, submitted his report, which stated "that there were about 40 men employed and all members of good standing average of wages per day $1.65 state of trade fair." Another shop steward reported that "he had tried all he could do to get the men to join the Union and has only met with abuse." Any cases of unfair dismissal were reported by shop stewards. Shop stewards for each firm were appointed at general meetings of the Local.

One of the major functions filled by the shop stewards was the enforcement of discipline. A visitor to Local 83 in the 1890s might have initially mistaken it for a police court. On 15 February 1893, a shop steward brought a charge against one Bro. Sellers for violating the Local's hours rules. Sellers admitted the charge "but Said in his defence that he had been doing a Job for him self at the time and that he never Worked for any boss After 5 O'clock...." The accused was tried before a trial committee, but its report was not judged satisfactory by the Local, and was sent back. Duly chastised, the Committee found Bro. Sellers guilty "of Violating the Trade rules of the Union," which verdict was confirmed at a general meeting, and the Secretary "was ordered to Notify bro Sellers to be present at Next Meeting to receive his sentence." On 4 April 1893, the President "reprimanded Bro Sellers ... and Cautioned Bro Sellers in the future." In the judicial system of Local 83, the principal punishment was the loss of esteem in the eyes of one's fellow workers.

Through the use of such instruments, Local 83 managed to improve conditions for the journeymen carpenters. Before 1889 the accepted union rate was $1.60 per hour in a ten-hour day. In 1889, in a major strike, the union won the nine-hour day and a 2¢ raise.

But the union's proudest achievement, the nine-hour day, was endangered in the 1890s. As early as 1891, James Dempster visited the union to explain that he could not compete with rural mills if his enterprise were forced to observe the nine-hour day. On 18 December 1894 the union instructed the recording secretary to inform McGuire in Philadelphia "that as Union 83 [is] in expectation of having trouble the Coming Winter with Dempsters & Co. Mill who are about to try and run their Mill 10 hours a day in the Spring and as we are determined to Stand by the 9 hours and fight the Mill if such Should take place and would ask what Course would be the best to pursue...." The ten-hour day at Dempster's began on 4 March 1895. Local 83 tried unsuccessfully to persuade the labour council to fight the new system. Such large employers as Rhodes, Curry & Co. and the Dominion and City governments continued to work 10 hours. There was a good deal of bitterness. After the 1895 Labour Day Parade, some members were put on trial for non-attendance, but one was found not guilty after he told the union "that he vowed he never would walk with A Man who worked 10 hours a day and otherwise he did not feel well enough to walk."

While such defeats divided journeymen carpenters, they also reinforced a sense of separateness, a sense that carpenters with any manliness would resist the temptations of the ten-hour employers. And many craft rituals reinforced this special collective sense. Attendance at funerals was expected and became, for a time in 1892, obligatory on penalty of a $1 fine. The carpenters socialized together. They opened a pool room in their quarters, formed a dancing class, and held card benefits for the indigent as well as nights of readings and recitations. (How temperate these gatherings were can only be guessed, but Local 83 was one of the few nineteenth-century Nova Scotia unions to reject prohibition, which might well have been another aspect of its struggles with the ATU.) Attempts to organize outside the boundaries of craft—for example, the efforts of the Workmen's Protection and Aid group amongst the Halifax unemployed in 1897—were coldly rejected. Even participation in the Labor Council, suspiciously associated with the ATU in the eyes of the Local, was curtailed after 1891.

Master carpenters played a significant role as members of the union in the 1890s. (Lessell himself probably had a small shop: he brought in a charge on 2 December 1890 against a fellow member for "spreading a report calculated to injure his business.") The master carpenters and the journeymen had, to a significant degree, the same interests: both masters and journeymen stood to lose if city wages and prices were undercut by externally based contractors and their ten-hour employees. The lengths to which Local 83 would go to placate these sympathetic masters were suggested by an incident in 1898, in which John Colp was charged with employing a man "who was considered not physically qualified to become a member of [the] Union." Colp, who employed over a dozen journeymen, represented the union in bargaining with employers. The investigating committee referred the question to the union, which swiftly initiated the man—in sharp contrast to the grilling it normally imposed on other candidates.

Craft rituals flourished. Local 83 paid $15 to acquire the banner from the 1860s so that it could be used once more in Labour Day Parades. In these parades, the union presented itself to the world. Its respect for tradition was suggested by the special treatment accorded the oldest members, always given a place of honour in the procession. "A discussion ... took place," we read in the minutes of 18 June 1890, "in reference to the advisability of procuring a band as so large a body as the carpenters' union would appear to great disadvantage without music...." Just what was to be worn in the Labour Day Parade was an issue that gave rise to vigorous, heated debates. A motion that the union wear white gloves on Labour Day passed in 1890, but only "after a very close contest." The competition for an official spot in the parade was so stiff that three ballots were necessary to elect the marshall for the 1895 procession.

The craft tradition within Local 83 had two distinct sides. Against other workers, non-unionists, unions pursuing different directions, it was a wall of exclusion. It was equally, as the nine-hours strike of 1889 revealed, a barrier on the frontier of control between masters and men. The most vivid evidence of this dual character of the craft tradition comes from the strikes waged by the union in its first decade.

The struggle for the nine-hour day was initiated throughout North America in the late 1880s. In Local 83, it started on 12 April 1889, when a resolution to demand the nine-hour day with ten hours pay was hotly debated. A motion that the carpenters should first consult with "the Carpenters outside of this Union and obtain their views in regard to the 9 hour movement" was defeated, as was an amendment that the nine-hour day be proclaimed as of 1 May 1889, with double time to be paid for any time over nine hours. After this inconclusive result, the two sides in the nine-hours debate tossed the question back and forth through several meetings. Finally the militants gained the upper hand. On 15 May 1889 a resolution "that on and after June 1st 1889 we demand 9 hours with an increase of 2 cts. per hour," was carried by a vote of 50 to 14. On 4 June 1889 the union wrote to McGuire at the International to find out what support the Brotherhood would give. McGuire's reply was read on 15 June 1889: it said the necessary aid would be given to the union. The union then set 18 June as the date for the inauguration of the new nine-hour system. Bosses who agreed to give the increase of 2¢ (which would bring the rate to about 19.5¢ per hour) and nine hours to every man in their employ, would not have their names published in the papers. Negotiations with the new Builders' Association (formed by employers in 1888 partly as a response to the new activism of construction workers) proved fruitless.

With military precision, about 120 journeymen walked off the job at the sound of the noon-day gun on 19 June 1889. Across the city, 13 major building firms noted the immediate impact of this strike. At S.M. Brookfield's, 38 or 40 carpenters protested the ten-hour day; at Mackintosh and McInnis, 50 men quit work on such sites as the Halifax Hotel; Alderman M.E. Keefe's 40 men were all idle, while James Dempster's men had won immediate concessions from the mill owner and were back at work. (He was soon to get his revenge.) The carpenters were successful across the board in their demands.

What did this strike of 1889 mean?

It suggested that, for the first time in Halifax, a polarization between employers and employed had taken place in the industry. On the side of the employers, the general contractors held out longer than the small masters (some of whom, out of sympathy or need, gave in very quickly). The general contractors dominated the Builders' Association, and when the union presented its demands in May, they went so far as to advertise for 100 strikebreakers to take the carpenters' places. All this suggested that the old, honoured idea of the unity of master and man was far less powerful than it had once been.

A new cohesion was also evident on the side of the workers. When the employers threatened them with strikebreakers, they in turn offered to furnish "first-class carpenters and joiners to finish any work required to be done for the approaching carnival, competent supervision supplied...." The journeymen saw themselves as part of a vast, international movement, and told the newspapers of the strength of the Brotherhood. "We are only one branch of the United Brotherhood," one carpenter explained, "which numbers over half a hundred thousand carpenters among its members. According to the rules only a certain number are allowed to strike at once. Our turn came this week, and we had to grasp the opportunity and make a demand on the bosses immediately." (According to early rules of the international union's constitution, only three strikes were to be waged at one time by the Brotherhood; in 1886 this had been reduced to two simultaneous strikes. The Brotherhood was to spend $300 on Halifax in 1889.)

These features—reliance on a large, international Brotherhood, and organized resistance from the employers—mark this as an "early modern" strike. But the 1889 strike was also the high point of the nineteenth-century style of craft unionism. It revealed that sense of exclusiveness and separateness without which, in a city like Halifax, the craft spirit could not survive.

For example, as many carpenters pointed out, a critical feature of the trade was the carpenter's ownership of his own tools and his role as the "brains of the building site." "It is admitted by every sensible man that the carpenter's craft requires more tools and a great deal more trained work than any of the other trades connected with building," remarked one carpenter, rather controversially. "Take for instance a recent case. The carpenters had to build a frame, a very careful and nice piece of work, for the stone masons to build a stone arch on; the masons, who simply piled the stones on the frame, received 20 cents an hour; while the carpenter, who did the designing and brain work of the job, got 17 cents an hour." "Look at the men who carry the hod and buy no tools at all," urged a strike poem:

> The mason with his hammer, trowel, and level to plum the wall,
> The tailor with a lap board, a tape, a goose, or two,
> A baker's kit is less than all. The clerk's pen, ink and rule,
> The plumber gets much better pay and buys less costly tools,
> And various trades too numerous to mention now to you.
> Are better paid than carpenters, and have less work to do.

The strike gave rise to a few new political initiatives—on 4 March 1890 a delegation waited on the local government with regard to the nine-hour day and in 1891 Premier W.S. Fielding was the guest of honour at a union function—but these represented no major change from the union's earlier position of gaining political support only in pursuit of its particular craft interests.

A lot of the cohesion on both sides evaporated after 1891. The Master Builders' Association, which had emerged as a result of the stresses of the late 1880s, folded in the 1890s. The union was also unable to sustain the unity needed to defend the nine-hour system, and divisions within both the union and the Labor Council undermined the achievements of 1889.

On 10 August 1891 Local 83 learned that the painters' union was fighting a battle with one employer against the large-scale introduction of apprentices. A vote to support the painters on strike was sustained unanimously, and Local 83 resolved to support the Labor Council in any action it decided to take. On 27 August 1891 Local 83 advised the Labor Council that it was "in favour of a Law that no Union men Work with non Union men and that bosses be notified." Carpenters working with painters from the firm in question now came out on a sympathetic strike (the first in the city of Halifax), which was co-ordinated by the Labor Council. The expenses of the strike, $110.00 per week, drove the union to request each member to loan the union $1 for its duration. Local 83 found itself in a dilemma, however, as individual members began to return to work, and it objected to the intransigence of the Labor Council, which, it felt, should have left the matter in the hands of the Painters' Union. After the strike ended in a compromise—an arbitration agreement which ruled out such sympathetic strikes in the future as well as imposing some limits on apprentices — demands were made in the union to withdraw from the Council altogether.

When, in 1892, the painters again went on strike over this same question, the Carpenters wrote to the Labor Council "That while Union 83 will assist the painters in every honourable and legal way, they are not in a position to go on strike against non Union painters...." When, in later disputes with Dempster's, the carpenters appealed to other building tradesmen not to work alongside non-union carpenters, they might have been reminded of their earlier inability to support the painters. It was typical of the city's craftsmen. Halifax craftsmen of the nineteenth century were not unified, and they pursued their separate craft traditions with far more enthusiasm than they showed for building a united labour movement.

The strikers of 1889 and 1891 looked both ways: to the future, certainly, in their struggle for nine hours, their affiliation with a much larger international organization, and their strong opposition to employers, but even more to the past, in their defence of the special prerogatives of this trade as against others, their alliance with the small masters who had once been trade unionists themselves, and in their reluctance to broaden the issues of this strike beyond the fairly narrow confines of the organized segment of their particular craft.

Partial mechanization, general contracting, and a widening gap between employer and employed had all changed the carpenters' craft in the nineteenth century. In many other respects, however, the world of the craftsmen had been modified but not transformed. The local craftsman still dealt with local employers, many of whom were still master carpenters, and he still saw the challenge facing the union as one of excluding the unskilled and the unmanly. He had limited dealings with the other building trades. There was as yet no visible "labour politics" and trade disputes were confined to very specific issues. There were important structural changes in the industry, but none had been of such scope as to destroy the traditional craft practices which the journeymen had evolved since the mid-nineteenth century. Only with the arrival of a new type of capitalism would Halifax carpenters face such a challenge.

2

The Craft Transformed
1900-1912

I tell you Brothers that I was actually ashamed of the very poor showing of members in fact it was one thing that marred the pleasure of the evening. I would suppose that the Revd. Gentleman would think that Unionism was at a discount in Halifax, and he is right. However I hope that things will take a turn for the better. It must be so, but not until the men wake up & realize the seriousness of their position which it seems they will not do until the iron heel of oppression is on their necks, when their families are in want, their neglected children in tatters walking the streets in semi-starvation then will they see the need of universal Unionism & rise as one man & demand their rights. Oh Brothers why not do it at once instead of...frittering away your time with delusions?

> — James Rosborough, Secretary of Local 83, reflects on poor attendance at a lecture and the crisis of the union in 1907.

Maritime social historians have long known that around the turn of the century—roughly from 1890 to 1910—a profound and far-reaching consolidation of capitalism transformed the economy of the region. In coal, steel, and cotton, once-independent companies were merged and merged again into ever-larger corporations, mostly controlled from Montreal.

What has been less noticed is the impact of this consolidation of capital on the skilled workers of the cities. It might be thought that such workers would have been sheltered from the shock of the transition. But if the building trades provide us with any indication, the opposite is true. Building craftsmen, no less than coal miners, faced this new consolidated capitalism at first hand. They built the company houses which dotted the coalfields, the large number of new institutions required by an expanding state, and the factories and port facilities required by this new phase of economic life. And very much like the coal miners, such urban craftsmen were forced to redefine many of their attitudes and habits of organization as they confronted this new structure.

The Halifax craftsmen had long struggled, with mixed results, against the incursions of outside *workers,* but they had not generally faced outside *employers.* A dramatic change took place in the building industry in the period 1890-1910: it became regional in scope and the small and medium-sized local contractors were shoved to its margins by much larger outside companies. Two outstanding examples of these new employers of building trades craftsmen were Rhodes, Curry & Co. and Silliker & Co.

Rhodes, Curry & Co., which the historian Nolan Reilly has shown to be very important to the working class in Amherst,[1] was the big company which most frequently threatened Local 83. According to a reminiscence in the *Herald* in 1917, the first construction contract entered into by the company was for the erection of Acadia College at Wolfville in 1878, and since then the company had built "many of the notable banks and public buildings in the Maritime Provinces." The company letterhead listed the company's many roles in 1913: "Building Contractors and Manufacturers of Doors, Sashes, Blinds, Mouldings, Kiln Dried Lumber, School, Office, Church & House Furniture and Building Materials Generally."

Rhodes, Curry won a large proportion of Halifax building contracts over the next two decades. The firm specialized in major institutional contracts. It became famous for building large stone structures, some as far afield as the United States. Across the region, it built the extension to the Intercolonial Railway roundhouse in Campbellton, fitted out the Kentville post office, the new court house in Sydney, and company housing for the Dominion Coal Company. In Halifax, Rhodes, Curry refitted the Nova Scotia Furnishing Company, built the new pier and sheds for the Intercolonial in 1898, as well as many private residences.

The firm was able to underbid local contractors, even for small projects in the Halifax area. In 1899, when the tenders were opened for the building of a barn on the grounds of the Mount Hope Asylum in Dartmouth, Rhodes, Curry won the $1,600 contract in preference to nine other tenders: three from Halifax, four from Dartmouth, and two from Truro. The company's success can be explained by its hold on excellent timber and stone resources in Cumberland County, its efficient use of machinery, and a large work force across the province. In 1901 alone the firm constructed 231 buildings.

A similar pattern applied to C.J. Silliker and Co., which, like Rhodes, Curry, exploited the potential of both construction and car-building.

Silliker began in 1885 and initially concentrated his efforts in Amherst, where he constructed a large percentage of the houses for that thriving town's population. In addition to building and contracting, it was noted in 1901, "Mr. Silliker runs a fully equipped wood-working factory, manufacturing all kinds of house finishing, lumber, etc., and making an extensive market for the raw lumber plentiful in this County." He employed 125 men during the construction season. Fire destroyed his works in 1906; shortly thereafter, to the annoyance of the Halifax labour movement, he came to Halifax.

Rhodes, Curry and Silliker were just two of a number of regional employers who emerged in the late-nineteenth century. They stood not only for a new way of organizing business; they represented an equally new way of organizing work.

These new men of the industry grew rich on the large number of massive public structures that were erected in the early twentieth century and the growth of a mass market for both company and private housing. Mechanization, prefabrication, and the use of new and inexpensive materials appealed to them. The Amherst Decoration and Flooring Company, for example, made up almost exclusively of Amherst businessmen, was formed in 1904 to manufacture flooring and tiling supposedly equal to marble in durability but far less expensive. The Queen's Hotel in Halifax, in which this new material was used extensively, was something of a show-case for other new building materials: here was a building almost completely made of brick, supported by steel girders, with its entire flooring of concrete and its walls of cement on expanded wire metal, all of which were thought to make the building as nearly fire-proof as possible. (It was later the site of a spectacular fire.) Another cheapening innovation (to which C.J. Silliker held the Maritime Provinces rights) was the use of painting and graining machines, which served to transform cheap clear cedar into wood which resembled the most expensive quartered oak, bird's eye maple, or French walnut.

The monuments to this era of the construction industry can still be seen in Halifax: such large, red-brick, graceless structures as the Forum, the old Technical College, Chebucto Road School, and the Armouries. The domestic housing erected by such Edwardian construction contractors was given very bad reviews when much of it collapsed in the Halifax Explosion. When the federal Commission of Conservation sought evidence of the "flimsy homes of Canada" for its Report on Fire Waste, it turned to Halifax, where, it noted, houses as far as two and a half miles from the scene of the Explosion were ripped apart like paper.[2] The notoriously inadequate company housing erected by these construction companies was probably not any worse than the cheap and shoddy dwellings they threw up in Halifax or wherever else a profit could be made.

Such men transformed not only the method of building, but the character of the labour market itself. Tramping—going from town to town on one's union ticket in search of a job—was a long and venerable method of providing relief for unemployed carpenters in both Britain and North America. Now, in the 1890s and early twentieth century, the pattern changed, as hundreds of building craftsmen migrated *within the region* in search of employment on the massive projects of the new age.

One striking example was the expansion of Sydney, to a great extent the work of Halifax craftsmen. "The Building Trades have been fairly busy, particularly among the carpenters. This is partly due at this season to the large number of mechanics having gone to Sydney," reported the Halifax correspondent of the *Labour Gazette* in 1901. (As a result of this building boom Local 943 in Sydney was reported in *The Carpenter* in April 1902 to be in a "thriving condition.") Another could be found in St. John's, Newfoundland, where in 1901 a controversy broke out over the arrival of Halifax building workers. According to the *Herald* of St. John's, after the great fire of 1892, an army of Halifax craftsmen, many employed by S.M. Brookfield, descended upon St. John's and worked at rebuilding the town. "With our usual lack of assertiveness," the *Herald* remarked bitterly, "we allowed them to make a fortune out of us." When rebuilding ceased, Brookfield brought some St. John's stonemasons back with him to Halifax, but "The Halifax union refused to allow them to work. The men offered to join the union, and the entrance was increased to keep them out. Mr. Brookfield, feeling himself bound to the men he had brought there, offered to pay the increased fee, and then the Halifax union showed its true colours—it refused to admit our men on any conditions." Why, asked the *Herald* in 1901, should Newfoundlanders now meekly assent to allow Brookfield to import "a horde of Halifax hod-carriers to build the new Court House, while our own tradesmen are excluded?"

The early twentieth century rings with cries like this one, as customary boundaries of craft and community were violated by new, integrated employers respectful of neither. What they imposed was a "free market in labour," which gave them access to much larger labour pools, but also robbed local craftsmen of protection.

The new employers left craftsmen with the worst of two worlds. Putting the wood supplies, stone supplies, planing mills, and sash and door works all under the control of one company did not solve workers' employment problems. No technical advance made craftsmen less dependent upon the weather. Large construction projects—the Sydney construction boom was the best example—could soften the blow of winter unemployment; in the winter of 1900-1901, Halifax carpenters told the *Labour Gazette* work was brisk, largely because of work in Sydney. But normally the building season extended from 1 May to the coming of winter conditions sometime in November. Although some finishing work could be done in winter, it provided far less employment than the building season. Bricklayers and stonemasons were the most dramatically affected of the building crafts, but carpenters and painters also were forced to contend with winter unemployment.

The impact of this seasonal rhythm of production can be seen in the timing of labour negotiations in the building trades. These customarily began in January or February and were concluded, either with a new wage schedule or a strike, on 1 May. Even if the climate did not absolutely forbid it, winter work was considered more costly. Renting customs were also a factor. People rented from the 1st of May, and there was a rush of work getting houses ready for that date; to a lesser degree the same was also true of the 1st of October. There was a rush of work in the spring and another in the fall. "These conditions result in throwing a considerable number of men in these trades out of work during the winter months," noted a 1910 provincial *Report* on the hours of labour. "During the winter these men must live upon their season's earnings, pick up odd jobs, or 'go to the woods.'" And because woodworking was concentrated outside Halifax, carpenters could not rely on bench work in winter to carry them through the dull months.

The new organization of production did not eliminate the small employer—he would linger until our own time in the construction industry—but it made his life a lot more precarious. Small masters easily became sweating sub-contractors under the underbidding pressure of a highly speculative and competitive market. Halifax building workers were deserted by one such marginal contractor in 1897, who absconded with $2,400 of the wages they had earned working on the Exhibition. The large projects also intensified the problem of instability. They attracted a much larger labour force in construction booms than could easily be supported in the inevitable slumps. In 1905, out of 98 stonemasons in Halifax, more than half were reported out of work in June. "This is very unusual for this season of the year," noted the *Herald*. "The men have always expected to be idle much of the winter, but to be out of work in June and with the prospect of nothing for the rest of the summer, is something almost unprecedented—is worse than any dullness experienced in years in Halifax. Some 24 men were engaged pointing the Armouries, and a number were engaged on the post office, but these works are complete and no new contracts are in sight...."

The emergence of much larger employers, in sum, did not bring stability to the labour market. It appears to have worsened the problem of casual labour. Workers found themselves at the mercy of under-capitalized and insecure sub-contractors or dependent on short-term arrangements with large building contractors. A much larger work force was tied more closely to the ebb and flow of market forces. Working for large employers thus meant losing a large measure of the pride of work and freedom associated with crafts, without a corresponding gain in economic reward or security.

The large, external contractors won a disproportionate share of the Halifax trade from 1900 to 1914. Just why Halifax contractors could not keep up with them mystified some contemporary writers. Looking at the major projects for 1913 alone, one commentator in the *Herald* reported that outside contractors were building the Technical College, the new Moirs factory, the largest public school project, the new Dalhousie College buildings, and many of the city's private residences. "Will any contractor tell me why it is that houses can be erected in this city by outside firms for less money than demanded by Halifax contractors?" he asked. "Both use Halifax labor. Therefore, the fault cannot be all due to our workmen.... In the larger field of building operations the outside contractor is 'putting it all over' the Halifax contractor, who [doesn't] even tender a bid. Outsiders take many of the big things and leave the little ones that [they do] not care to take chances on...."

One difference, the commentator suggested, lay in the intensity of supervision over the labour process. When the outside contractors started building, they placed a qualified overseer on the site, while Halifax contractors thought that the work would go on all the same without such constant supervision. It was a telling observation, suggesting the sweeping changes that the new consolidated economy was bringing to the world of the Halifax carpenters.

These structural changes in the economy entailed a direct challenge to the craft principles which had guided the organization of Halifax carpenters since the mid-nineteenth century.

Restrictive hiring, apprenticeship, and cordial relations between masters and journeymen had once guaranteed acceptance of the carpenter as a skilled craftsmen; now these skills were placed in question by machinery, casualism, and the rise of the foreman. Craftsmen once central to the building industry were now shoved unceremoniously to its margins. As the historian Wayne Roberts finds in the case of Toronto building craftsmen in the same period, modernizing contractors moved to undermine the rounded and monopoly-bestowing skills of artisans in order to establish broken-down specializations, many of them less skilled and lower paid. Like their Toronto counterparts, but perhaps to an even greater extent, Halifax carpenters experienced these structural changes as an assault upon their living standards and their self-conception as craftsmen.

The same consolidation of capitalism which concentrated ownership and control entailed fragmentation and disorganization in the labour market. Employers now required more men at their beck and call in order to complete the large institutional projects of the day, but the impact of this was to increase the number of men who, dependent on such short-term projects, were reduced to the status of casual (while nonetheless skilled) workers.

The new structures entailed endemic unemployment and insecurity, all the more so after the closing of the Imperial Dockyard in 1905. The Dockyard had been a major source of stable employment for as many as 300 Halifax workingmen, a number of them carpenters. The poverty and distress of unemployed members haunted the proceedings of Local 83. "Sorely afflicted" members had their cards kept clear by the union during their time of distress.

The traditional seasonal fluctuations in the industry aggravated this problem. As revealed in the 1910 report on the Hours of Labour, one Halifax contractor employed 50% fewer men in winter than in summer, while others virtually ceased operations altogether in the winter months. S.M. Brookfield, one of the largest unionized employers in the city, paid out $1,906.35 and $1,915.95 in wages during the winter in two 14-day periods about the year 1909, and $4,607.75 and $4,016.50 during two similar periods in the summer. The same contractor told an arbitration board in 1901 that he employed about 20 men all through the year; sometimes he had as many as 50 and at other times 100 carpenters. William Sullivan, a journeyman, told the board that carpenters did not average more than 175 working days a year. While hypothetically indus-trialization might have held out the promise of providing more work year-round because standardized articles could be stockpiled, in practice woodworking mills closely followed the building season and were usually located at some distance from Halifax.

The trade union had no permanent solutions to the problems of sea-sonal and general unemployment. It did try a number of both short-term and long-term approaches. Make-work projects, concessions to large employers in exchange for security of employment, out-migration, and taxation of outsiders coming to Halifax to work were all put forward in this period.

Make-work projects were often suggested. In 1905, one activist urged the union to get jobs for union members from the city's Exhibition Committee. Another, more controversial proposal was to relax the union's nine-hour standard and give members access to the jobs offered by the larger, ten-hour contractors. When unemployment reached crisis proportions in 1910, one member called on 18 January 1910 for the softening of union rules "which gave to the non-union men the bulk of what ever was going these times, to the detriment and discomfiture of the union man." Under this member's plan, union men would be allowed to work for ten hours a day for such new employers as Silliker. "[A]s some union men were not in a position to be idle for any length, [he] thought it was the duty of the union to allow such to get work if possible ... and thought it would be more than likely the means of organizing and inducing other workmen to join Local Union #83." Negotiations with the employer on this strategy, which included bringing Silliker into the union hall to outline his position, ran into grave difficulties. Silliker, who approached the Local to negotiate hours and wages prior to opening his Halifax works, lost whatever favour he might thus have won by literally slamming his door in the face of the union's president. The minutes note on 15 February 1910: "The Bros. present thought that, that indignity offered to one of the Union, should remind us that we could not expect any great sacrifice on the part of Mr. Silliker, but that we should keep our lamps upon him, and get speech with the directors when ever possible." So ended Local 83's attempt to win a foothold in factory woodworking through concessions. Its willingness to consider such concessions was striking evidence of its diminished position. Some union members, forced to choose between union rules and making a living, quietly violated their union obligations.

Carpenters could always turn to another response to unemployment— tramping to another city. Yet there were obstacles here as well. Problems such as those which faced the Halifax workers also faced carpenters across the United States, who responded by doing their utmost to keep outside craftsmen away. Some members of Local 83 did exercise their option of going to the West or New England, but (if the minutes are any guide) they were not that numerous.

Or carpenters could seek legislated protection in the local labour market. On 21 January 1902, they pressed upon the Halifax and District Trades and Labor Council the idea of taxing "Persons coming in to the City to work on Contract or Dispose of made up Goods etc." On 15 December 1903 the Local proclaimed its complete opposition to the Mayor's cherished tax-reform schemes unless he came up with a clause granting protection to Local 83 from outside labour.

In the absence of industrial standards legislation, however, urban craftsmen had little protection against the lower standards of wages and hours of rural workers. S.M. Brookfield made that brutally clear in an interview with the *Chronicle* in 1901. If Halifax wages went up, he said, "the Builders would have to get men from outside of the city to do the work or else give up business.... The men outside of the city work ten hours a day, and a large portion of the doors and sashes are made in the country towns and sold in the city." He added that he could buy doors and sashes more cheaply than he could manufacture them.

The dilemma of the Halifax carpenters was that they were surrounded by thousands of rural woodworkers, some of them carpenters, others handymen capable of many types of wood work. As a survey carried out by the federal Department of Labour revealed, their unions, in the few places they existed, were weak; their wages and conditions, poor.

In 1904, Amherst carpenters working for Rhodes, Curry were paid between 14 and 17½¢ per hour for a 10-hour day (9½ on Saturdays). They were paid $1.75 per day in Antigonish and worked 10 hours per day, 6 days a week. (Their wages had last advanced, according to the survey, in 1870!) From Clark's Harbour in 1901, the ability of the carpenters outside Halifax to combine various occupations was revealed by one carpenter in his rather rough-hewn note to the Department of Labour. "The wages hear for good carpenters have been very small as our season is very short," he wrote, adding, "some years we done 5 months which brings much distress to some of our carpenters as for myself I do all kinds of work in the carpenters line boat building brick laying occasionally on vessels almost anything that comes along some of our carpenters are forced to go abroad until the lobster season is closed."

In North East Margaree the rates ran from 9¢ to 15¢ per hour with a ten-hour day and were said to have increased steeply in recent times. In Middleton, the wages were slightly better, at $2 to $2.50 per day. In New Waterford, another roughly-hewn letter informs us, "the Dominion Coal Co. is indavering to keep the wages as low posable they are Sending Agents out through the Countrys after carpenters promising a good rate of wages." Over 100 carpenters could be found in the vicinity at the turn of the century. In Parrsboro, the correspondent noted that "There has not been any change in labour or in time or wages, for the last ten years in this part of Nova Scotia," which meant that carpenters were earning 15¢ per hour in 1904. (By way of comparison, rates in Halifax for tradesmen were 25¢ and for "rough hands" 22¢, both for a nine-hour day in 1904.)

It is easy, working with the records of the Halifax union, to see these rural men only through the eyes of the trade unionists trying to keep them out. But, of course, such rural skilled workers were often miserably exploited, and their pursuit of many occupations at the same time gave them almost no security. They were unable to reform the conditions of their work.

Trade unions were scarce. As a correspondent from Middleton told the Department of Labour, "We work ten hours for a day. No union of 8 Hours Here. We Have no union of any Kind in Nova Scotia or in Annapolis County." "In Yarmouth," reported the correspondent, "we have no Unions, we work all week if we have it to do." Remarked another correspondent from the same town, "I beg to say that in Yarmouth unions are unknown, workmen go on after the old Style, a day[']s work is 10 hours.... there is no Standard of wages, all Seems to be governed by the demand."

W.L. Oliver, a crusty old shipbuilder in Digby, provided a rare insight into attitudes towards unions in the mind of a traditional artisan in his reply to the Department's questionnaire in 1904. "The only remarks I can make [are] ... I am not in sympathy with Labour Unions & ... My way, would be to serve the Bosses or leaders [of unions] the way that ... I've got rid of stray dogs in New York i.e. put them in a wire cage & lower them off of a wharf. I am an old ship builder built ships in U.S.A. before the civil War & have never struck a Labor Union. *I hate the name.*"[3]

Obviously organizing the carpenters of the South Shore, Valley and other areas was going to pose some interesting problems. The Brotherhood sent W.J. Shields, an organizer, up to Nova Scotia to undertake this work in 1907 and 1908, and he filed fascinating reports in *The Carpenter* from January to December, 1907. He organized a local union in Yarmouth, and observed the organization of Local 1538 in Bridgetown, a union said to be "small in numbers, but big in reasoning force; it comprises a set of men who are sufficiently intelligent to stand together to the effect of a nine-hour work day and a $2.25 minimum wage, a condition [which], while small, is beyond that enjoyed by any other community for miles around." In Middleton he interviewed the local carpenters "and learned that in the town is a large trim plant, the owner of which is strongly prejudiced against unions. He not only dictates the conditions of the men employed, but prescribes penalties of expulsion to him who dares to oppose his will. He owns the men, and from what I could learn, they agree to the ownership." In Lunenburg, the organizer met sympathetic carpenters, but found that they insisted on getting their employer's sanction before organizing, which he was unable to obtain.

Shields made some interesting comments about the general position of the Brotherhood in the Maritimes. He argued that the climate was a retarding factor. "Using the testimony of some of the residents, they sum it up to this effect—eight months of winter and four months of summer," he wrote. "the custom prevails to attend to the wants in our line in these four months, or possibly six, and considering the meager earnings in this short season of work, it introduces an environment that robs the individual of his natural ambition, which leads to a slow consideration of the necessity of organization." Single-industry communities were also a problem. He reported that in such communities the corporations exercised "a general control over not only the affairs of local business, but the affairs of men as well. Their dictation is generally accepted, and it is apt to be not particularly favorable to organized labor." Finally, he looked at the large numbers of rural carpenters. "Then, again, the communities having a sufficient carpenter population to support a union are scattered far apart.

The territory between contains many of what [are] styled ... "farmer carpenter[s]," but out of the reach of our organized efforts."

It was an unhappy situation for carpenters trying to defend their craft by traditional exclusivist methods. If wages in Halifax went up, a ready supply of men could be brought in from the countryside. Even worse, with the new vertically integrated companies drawing upon workers from the rural areas and industrializing many aspects of production, the standards of the industry increasingly were drawn from these lower-paid workers. For many good reasons, carpenters defended a craft tradition they had carried with them from the eighteenth century, but to do so meant trying to build protective walls around the city at the very time that the new consolidated capitalism was eroding any such barriers. The carpenters could hope, as the arbitration board put it in July, 1901, that the improvement in hours and wages they had won "will not be confined simply to the city of Halifax, but will make itself felt more or less throughout the Province, and that in the result the city contractors will not find themselves any more heavily handicapped than they are at the present." Unfortunately for them, however, it was more likely that influences would flow the other way.

Even efforts to maintain the closed shop, partially successful in the nineteenth century, were less so in the twentieth. One big difficulty was the sheer diversity of employers now hiring carpenters. Carpenters found themselves doing a large amount of shipwork, because the local shipwrights and caulkers had declined in response to the diminished opportunities for new ship construction (as opposed to a continuing demand for wooden ship repair). Employed in such contrasting locations as the cotton factory, the docks, and the small workshops, carpenters had difficulty in even monitoring their employment position, let alone changing it. The largest contractors, like Rhodes, Curry — who might have given Local 83 the unifying experience of working for large employers — tended to avoid hiring Halifax trade unionists unless forced to do so. The carpenters could do little to stabilize the construction labour market. Although there were interesting anticipations of the "hiring hall" in Local 83 (such as the resolution of 2 October 1900 calling for erection of a board to list the names of out-of-work members, and the occasional reading of a request for skilled carpenters from outside contractors), the Local had no direct role in hiring.

Clearly the strategies which had served well in a small and protected urban craft achieved at best mixed results in the new economy. As employers made clear in strikes in 1901 and 1903, there was an abundance of rural workers who were happy to work ten hours a day in woodworking shops and on building sites. One possible strategy could have been to organize all the woodworkers, skilled and unskilled, within the craft union. The International was in this period anxious to extend its sovereignty in this way and create a large "empire in wood."[4] The admission of millmen was discussed on 11 February 1911 in connection with workers at the Nova Scotia Car Company. It was deemed advisable to admit them to the union, in accordance with the General Constitution, but the sticking point was the admission of men who worked ten hours. The craftsmen of Local 83 were divided on this question, and only after the International's intervention did the Brotherhood in the Maritimes undertake the general organization of woodworkers.

Thus Local 83 was reduced to the position of representing a minority of the carpenters, and, worse, a minority in the least dynamic and prosperous sector, the small local masters and contractors. Shields, writing on his visit, put the best face on the situation. He noted in *The Carpenter* in December, 1907, that "while Local 83 might be stronger numerically, still there is a satisfaction in the fact that all the most skilled men of the craft are in the union. This makes it possible for this membership to control the best jobs in the city." Still, the Halifax carpenters had fallen behind. "The carpenters of Halifax should be enjoying the eight-hour day; also a higher wage than [is] now paid, and would enjoy these privileges if a higher standard of organization could be reached."

Yet even in the "best jobs" with certain employers, where the union claimed a monopoly on the jobs through the closed shop, it achieved something less in practice. S.M. Brookfield's was one firm Local 83 claimed to have organized; indeed, when carpenters applied for work there, they had to give bonds as to their intention of becoming union members at the first available opportunity. But even at Brookfield's, the number of non-unionists seemed to increase without Local 83 being able to do much about it. In James Dempster's firm, where the union had forced a quick capitulation to the nine-hour day in 1889, the union saw a mirror image of its own weakness: by 1903 Dempster was a non-union employer, who (the Minutes noted disapprovingly on 14 May 1903) "put up stairs on Union jobs ... employing Scabs to do the work." The frustration of union men emerges from this description, from the Minutes of 20 June 1911, of work in the city's North End: "Reference was made to the new curling rink now in course of erection on Agricola St., and that it was a scab job in every particular, with only one union man employed. On the other hand there were employed, non-union men, ex-union men, and suspended and expelled members the whole outfit going to show a first class scab job. Again those living in the vicinity were for a long time refused as much as a shaving from off the job." The union's inability to stop the unfair discharge of its members stemmed from its failure to control hiring. So too did the union's apparent inability to discipline its members effectively, to prevent them from taking work thought to be outside the domains of the craft (such as laying floors or roof boards, opposed partly on the grounds that such jobs were paid for on a piecework basis), or even from having their own homes constructed by non-unionists.

A striking example of the union's inability to enforce craft controls (and of its continuing wish to do so) could be found in 1911. Local 83 followed the career of one Emmerson, a fiercely anti-union foreman who appeared bent on breaking the nine-hour rule. "It was interesting to note the proceedings of this particular gentleman, how easily he could fly from coop to coop, and the opinion of the meeting was, that his wings would need clipping," noted the secretary on 17 October. It was hoped that union men working at the present site of Emmerson's activities, a project of the local firm of Falconer & McDonald, "could easily determine Mr. Emmerson's course" (put bluntly, run him off the site). They evidently succeeded in doing so, for the unpopular foreman was next found on Pier No. 9, the Local advising members there on 5 December 1911 to keep "Mr. E. on the move." Emmerson then hired himself out as a first-class bricklayer, and the secretary noted that "it was to be hoped he would be kept busy." However, carpenters at the King Edward Hotel project reported that Emmerson had once more emerged as a boss at the site and was working men ten hours per day at a low rate of 24¢ per hour. There was a note of grim satisfaction in the secretary's comment on 21 November that "Through the efforts of union men Mr. E. had been made flit from job to job sooner than he would become a union member," and in his speculation that the "ballot box would a tale unfold" should Emmerson ever seek to apply for membership in the Union. Yet the hard facts were that the union had merely managed to inconvenience Emmerson, not put him out of business, and his activities pitted the unionists who resigned themselves to working for him against those who spurned such employment. And if the union encountered such difficulties *within* the local, craft-oriented sector, we can well imagine what had happened to any control over foremanship outside it.

No trace remains in the local records of enforcement of apprenticeship regulations; such debates as occurred over apprentices involved their position in the Labour Day Parade. Quite possibly some of the local firms continued to honour restrictions on the numbers and training of apprentices, and informal traditions of teaching carpentry to youths persisted well into the twentieth century. (Brookfield's traditionally hired youths to work in the sash and door mill, and then gradually introduced them to outside work. In this and other respects this firm's traditionalism favoured the craft union.) However, firm rules concerning apprentices were not found in the industry as a whole.

The inability of the carpenters to protect themselves in the labour market reflected their inability to do much to improve their position in the workplace. Industrial accidents were common; the Local's minutes on 5 February 1907 and 6 February 1912 report cases such as that of Bro. Janes, badly injured, who was the sole support of a wife and five small children, or that of "the family of the unfortunate young man who was hurt on the Moirs job and who died shortly afterward." The snapping of a derrick at the Woodside Sugar Refinery in 1912 killed three of S.M. Brookfield's men, who fell 60 feet amid a whirl of flying steel and wood. The first report of the Nova Scotia Workmen's Compensation Board revealed that, outside coal and steel, the highest number of claims was found in construction. Scaffolding was not rigorously inspected, and the new, high buildings of the early twentieth century entailed greater risk of fatal falls for the workers who built them.

Carpenters were able to win back the nine-hour day in strikes in 1901 and 1903. Unfortunately, although such victories were important, they were also easily eroded. Carpenters working for the increasingly dominant outside contractors worked the same ten-hour day as the workers in the woodworking factories. Some of Local 83's members saw insistence on the nine-hour rule as a roadblock to winning influence among the millmen and other ten-hour workers. It was clear that the general contractors were setting the provincial standards in the industry, as the provincial *Report of the Commission on Hours of Labour* noted in 1910:

> There are throughout the Province many woodworking establishments, apart from the lumber mills. They vary in size from small sash and door factories, employing a few men, to the Rhodes, Curry Company, which employs over 800 men. The working day, as a rule, is ten hours, though in Halifax and Yarmouth, there are firms that have a nine hour day. Many of the smaller places do a business which is local, limited, and affected by the seasons, or by fluctuations in the building trades. These small firms would be seriously affected by an eight hour law. They compete with difficulty against the larger firms. Their total turnover in each case is small, and an increase in cost would probably hasten what appears to be the tendency in favor of larger companies.

Within the building trades proper, the provincial standard day was ten hours, with "many" in Halifax and Sydney reporting a nine-hour day, and the Halifax bricklayers, alone in the building trades, working only eight. It appears from the minutes of Local 83, however, that even within the confines of the city's unionized carpenter shops, the nine-hour day was often violated. Local 83 on 3 August 1909 gave "grave and serious consideration" to the firms "doing business in our midst, who were working their help contrary to our by-laws and trade rules," and to the fact "that there were two or more members of ours who were thus violating their obligation." The problem can readily be appreciated: local contractors being underbid by larger concerns working a ten-hour day would be sorely tempted to extend their own hours of labour and thus to cheapen the price of labour.

Exactly the same problem arose with the defence of the standard rate at which carpenters were paid. As the contractor M.E. Keefe suggested to the *Chronicle* on 20 June 1901, although carpenters logically might be expected to receive the same pay as stonemasons, "There are more of the former and they are more easily obtained for work, and he supposed that was the reason they did not get as much pay." The union did negotiate standard rates of pay in the industry, but was forced to make numerous exceptions for impoverished and unemployed members.

When the supply of labour exceeded demand, collective discipline was difficult to maintain. In one specific case reported in the Minutes of 19 March 1912, involving the construction of the King Edward Hotel, complaints made by one brother about the job's low wages "were carried on the wings of the morning to those in charge of the 'Edward' job, and the brother was informed shortly after that his job was vacant." Then two other union members accepted positions on the site at a lower rate than that considered unsuitable by the discharged member. As the secretary noted, "These statements certainly created quite a hub bub, and why not, when one brother quit a job when seeking for better conditions, two other brothers would fill his place for less money and longer hours." Such events reveal the union's difficulties in specific instances in enforcing standards and preventing members from underbidding each other.

Although general rates were set in a strike in 1903, there was almost a decade before the next general setting of rates, during collective negotiations in 1912. In this long interval, and in the absence of any machinery for collective bargaining, the "standard rate" was not rigorously maintained. Local 83 won an increase from 18¢ per hour to 22¢ per hour in 1901, but in 1903 was forced to submit to an arbitration award which differentiated between skilled and experienced mechanics (who were given 25¢), and the less skilled men (who were left at 22¢). The carpenters attempted to take the rate paid by the federal government, 30¢ in 1911, as *the* minimum standard, but many contractors and the City of Halifax itself paid less. Under the threat of a strike, the minimum was pushed up to 32¢ in 1912 and to 35¢ after the strike of 1913. Halifax carpenters were paid roughly at the same rate as Toronto carpenters until the latter's organizing efforts widened the gap in 1912. In short, the carpenters were able to win large strikes, but were often unable to enforce the gains thus established.

The failure to set standard rates stemmed partly from the anarchy prevailing among the employers. Often these men were not even easily located. In response to the workingmen's agitation, builders had created the Builders' Association in 1889; by 1901 the employers' voice was styled the Manufacturers' and Master Mechanics' Association, a group which controversially claimed direct descent from the 1889 body. According to remarks of contractor M.E. Keefe published in the *Chronicle* on 20 June 1901, the group in 1901 was practically disorganized, "as it had no head, and no meetings were called." The Minutes of 6 April 1909 tell the same story. In pursuit of the 30¢ minimum standard, "Bro Hemming chairman of [the union] committee appointed to wait on Mr. Freeman, Sect.y of Builders Association trying to make a date and to have a committee from aforesaid association meet a like committee from carpenters union failed to connect, Mr. Freeman stating that he had no authority to arrange for a meeting with our committee." The Association later replied that "owing to the disorganized state of the Builders Association it would be impossible to obtain a committee from the Builders."

One of the central tasks of trade unionism was to attempt to bring some order into the ranks of the contractors. The union was repeatedly frustrated in its attempts to deal with them. Members were told in 1912 that the employers now had an organization comprised of 22 members, which caused the secretary to remark sarcastically on 24 January, "This news from the president was quite a revelation to those assembled, when it was well known that when we were asking for 30¢ per hour, the word came to us emphatically that there was no such an organization as an Employers' association. The brothers assembled in solemn conclave doubted very much if there was any such an organization as an Employers' Association, but thought before the middle of March we would surely know for certain." Workingmen were frustrated in their strike in 1913 by the difficulty of meeting with an employers' committee with real bargaining power. The unionized employers dominating the employers' association did not make up a majority of local contractors. Fragmented because they were bidding against each other, and divided between the large and secure firms and the small and desperately marginal, the contractors may also have avoided forming a strong negotiating body because they could plead disorganization whenever workingmen requested more money.

It was difficult for workingmen to organize effectively in such an industry. Certainly schemes for permanent collective bargaining had been tried. The Manufacturers' and Master Mechanics' Association charged in 1901 that the striking carpenters were in violation of an 1890 agreement which imposed heavy penalties if the union ordered its men out before efforts were made to effect a settlement. The carpenters replied by noting that this agreement between the Amalgamated Trades Union and the Master Mechanics' Association could hardly be considered binding given that both bodies had since collapsed and been reorganized under other names, and that the agreement only applied, in any case, to the Painters' Union. Since the employers dropped the argument and never pressed for penalties, one can safely assume that the union's case was a strong one.

Although an "Arbitration Committee" was reported in the *Acadian Recorder* of 26 May 1891, "the purpose of which was to endeavor to prevent or arrange any difficulties or misunderstandings arising between employers and employees, during the current year," the committee failed to survive the year of its birth.

The carpenters' major strike in 1901 was settled by a five-man Board of Arbitrators, under provincial industrial arbitration legislation. As part of the award, the arbitrators laid down rules for the future governance of the trade: "That should any difficulty or dispute arise in the future between carpenters and master builders, which cannot be settled by the parties themselves, such difficulty or dispute should be promptly submitted to arbitration without suspension of work." But arbitration, in either its modern or its nineteenth-century meaning (orderly collective bargaining assisted by a third party) never became a feature of the daily life of the trade in this period. It initially held attractions for workingmen, because it suggested that employers would at least have to meet them collectively; it was subsequently tarnished with an anti-labour brush in 1903, so much so that Local 83 was among the first labour bodies in Canada to pronounce itself opposed to the federal version of industrial disputes legislation in 1908.

Failure to handle day-to-day grievances with employers was paralleled by inability to organize effectively in the workplace. The nineteenth-century network of shop stewards had fallen into disarray by the first decade of the twentieth. Although the Local resolved on 6 May 1902 "That a Shop Steward be appointed in every Firm in the City," the appointment of shop stewards took place only on 14 May of the following year. Shop stewards were appointed on 26 July 1910, and new elections were held on 4 July 1911, when it was recorded that since it had been a while since the stewards had been appointed, such offices ought to be looked into. Shop stewards were appointed for seven places of employment in 1911, with the understanding that they were to be remunerated for time lost in the discharge of their duties. The pattern was one of spotty and ineffectual performance. In contrast, for example, with such bodies as the "managing committee" in the coal mines, shop stewards rarely brought day-to-day grievances to the attention of the union and far fewer issues were resolved through the trials of members. A fine of $30 was imposed for working on Labour Day; a brother who lived by his creed that "he would leave the Union before he would quit [work] at 5 o'clock" was fined $5.00 on 5 February 1910 despite his plea of "extenuating circumstances"; two other brothers were found not guilty of an unnamed offence "in the absence of direct evidence." Compared to the cases tried in the nineteenth century (or with the huge volume of such cases tried regularly in the mining unions), the record was unimpressive.

Menaced by free trade in labour and anarchy among the employers, the carpenters faced an even more serious structural problem in the challenge posed by the new emerging economy to the very definitions of skill in carpentry.

This was the major theme of the negotiations between employers and employees in 1901-1903. The arbitration award of 1901 set "the rate of wages payable to carpenters" at 22¢ per hour as of 1 August. The builders vigorously objected to it. "They say," reported the *Chronicle* of 12 July 1901, that "they regret ... the arbitrators did not take time to distinguish the difference between a joiner and a carpenter, and fix, at least, two rates. They claim that the award means that a Halifax carpenter would receive forty per cent higher wages than the average price paid throughout the Province, and that inferior men would receive about twenty per cent more than the best joiners at St. John." An accompanying letter from the builders in the same issue argued that if 22¢ was to be the minimum hourly rate for a day of nine hours, "we are sorry for the second-class men, because we could not afford to employ them, that is if we are to carry out our agreement, which we wish to do, or until March, '02, at least." Referring to the competition from outsiders, the Halifax builders remarked, or rather threatened: "We also wish to know if outside parties coming in to do work will be asked to pay the same rate of wages that we pay, so to put us on a level. We were not on a level before by from 19 to 20 per cent as regards the manufacture of all the finish entering into the carpenter's and joiner's work of building. And now if your rate is to be adopted we will still further be handicapped by 22¼ per cent, so you see we must close up our mills and workshops for the manufacture of wood-work and depend entirely upon outsiders for the same. The City carpenters and joiners would then merely fix it in place." Responding to these criticisms of the Manufacturers' and Master Mechanics' Association, the arbitrators said that 22¢ was "no more than a fair remuneration for carpenters who devote their energies and their skill with zeal to the services of their employers," but added these remarks on the question of skill:

> They [the arbitrators] think ... that the Executive of the Carpenters' Union should exercise care and see to it that only properly qualified carpenters are admitted to membership in the Union.
>
> They consider that men to whom the name of "hatchet-and-saw-men" can properly be applied, should be classed under the head of "unskilled labor" and their wages determined accordingly.

But how was this line to be drawn? In 1903, when the union's demand for a universal minimum rate of 25¢ per hour was referred to an arbitration board, the arbitrators ruled on 24 June "that an increase to 25 cents per hour would be justifiable in regard to all members of the Carpenters' Union who are skilled and experienced mechanics," and expressed the opinion that a large number of union members were entitled to this rate. Then it added a crucial qualification.

> It has been alleged however that there are some carpenters belonging to the Union who have not the necessary skill and training to entitle them to this higher rate of 25 cents per hour and the Arbitrators therefore recommend that wherever any difference of opinion may exist between an employer and any carpenter in his employ as to the skill of the said employee the question of his skill shall be determined by a reference to the foreman under whose immediate supervision the carpenter may be working or in the case of future applications for work by any foreman of an employer who may be in charge of the particular branch of work at which the applicant desires to be engaged, the decision of such foremen in all cases to be given promptly and to be accepted as final while the man continues in that employment. Said foreman in deciding such matter must be free from interference by either of the parties to this arbitration. Any such interference will be considered a violation of the terms of this decision. Said foremen must not be members of the Carpenters' Union. In the event of any foreman declining to decide the question of the skill of the workman then such foreman and his employer shall mutually agree upon a competent third person whose decision must be accepted as conclusive.[5]

It was an alarming decision, because it removed the union from any position of power in an area decisive to the very self-definition of craftsmen.

Under the award, a number of the men were rated at 22¢. On 6 July the Local held a special meeting to decide "what action this Union would take on the action of the bosses in not paying the rate awarded by arbitration, thereby violating the decision of the arbitrators ... [A]fter a lengthy & very explicit statement of the case Moved seconded ... that the Master Builders get notified that if they do not pay the 25 cts. per an hour after 24 hours notice that This Union will declare a strike...." The strike vote carried 71-3 with 10 abstentions. A communication from the general secretary of the international union in reference to the arbitration said that the local men had been unfairly dealt with "& that our Union had every right to refuse to agree to it."

The 1903 strike, fought on the issue of the definition of skill, was a decisive defeat for the union. In June *The Carpenter* reported that Local 83 had received the Board's sanction for a strike, the question of financial support to be taken up as emergencies required. On 7 July Local 83 set up a committee to have a legal document drawn up "for the Bosses to sign agreeing to pay 25 cts per hour & to keep their time so that they be paid for their services." Only the small master carpenters signed the agreement; a larger employer coolly informed Local 83 "that there were no skilled men in the City."

The strike which ensued (lasting from 9 July to 17 August, bringing out 160 carpenters in 20 establishments) was permeated with bitter charges that the master carpenters were destroying the craft and deceiving the public. As Local 83 put it in one letter, published in the *Chronicle* on 21 July 1903, "The Master Builders declared before the arbitration that they were unwilling to pay twenty five cents per hour to all men, they have nevertheless been paying that amount to every man they can fetch from the country, many of whom are incompetent to perform the work required of them, while our own men, residents and taxpayers of the City, and wholly competent to perform any work required of them, are shut out altogether from employment, and the public are being imposed upon by having their work done by such men, and that it is very unjust to the public and the carpenters. The public are actually paying to unskilled men the wage asked for by the Union. They are also having their work botched by the action of the employers in hiring such help...." On 13 August, a dispirited Local voted to call off the strike by a vote of 38-24.

This defeat marked a turning point in the history of Halifax craftsmen: the critical line between skilled and unskilled was henceforth to be drawn not by journeymen relying on their own assessment of the skill of a fellow worker, but by foremen deploying the criteria of their employers. Of course, the union attempted to impose its own definitions of skill by initiating only those members who, it was satisfied, were qualified craftsmen. (On 19 March 1912, for example, an application from a man who "had been but two years only at the craft" was ordered to a full stop. "The President here called the attention of the Financial Secretary to ... the General Constitution, and few and short were the words that were used.") But such measures could not conceal the fact that the decisive defences of craft had been breached. During the strike of 1913, carpenters were menaced by strikebreakers—not only the rural craftsmen, but long-shoremen and labourers hiring themselves out as carpenters as well.

Exclusivism as a technique of organizing the craft was no longer an effective approach, yet the Halifax craftsmen had little to put in its place. For these craftsmen, the erosion of traditional boundaries and standards seemed to signal the end of the old, but it was only with the most hesitant and reluctant steps that they adapted to the new.

These changes in the craft meant that trade unionism itself faced a serious challenge in the early twentieth century. Local 83 in 1912 had roughly the same number of members as it had had in 1901. No significant progress was made in expanding the range of the organization or bringing it to new kinds of workers. This was in marked contrast to the international pattern, which was one of very rapid growth.[6]

Until 1912, one has an impression of a small and somewhat lethargic group. Meetings were often sparsely attended affairs: How could one take seriously the protests of members over constitutional change? the secretary asked on 20 June 1911, "When one takes into consideration that there were only twelve members present, and the average attendance at meetings would in all probability total no more than twenty members, and it is the same twenty who were present at all the meetings...."

As the evidence of the union's weakness mounted, so did controversy within the union, especially after 1910, as more impatient rank-and-file members clashed with a cautious executive. As described by the often sarcastic pen of the secretary, debates were to become "rather hot and personal," as on 1 March 1910. At the next meeting on 22 March, when the Local came to discuss a questionnaire from international headquarters regarding its demand for sanction to go on strike, the secretary observed, "It would be needless for your secretary to chronicle that the 15 questions could be answered amicably. No matter how small a gathering there [were] almost sure to be [dissensions]. Our meeting was no exception to the general rule, but notwithstanding passed over without blood letting...." As the year went on, the debates grew more impassioned. The secretary noted that "a talk of not much importance was engaged in" on 27 April, "some of it not very edifying or elevating." Three days later, he noted a very stormy meeting, "one of the most lively and interesting ... which had occupied the attention of the members for some time past," and "through the stress of circumstances, and cross firing quibbles the president was forced to vacate the chair and retire from [the] meeting room." The debate became even more bitter when former President Ira Mason laid unspecified charges against the Local's president on 17 May 1910. "Now it was every brother's opportunity to spout," the secretary said of one debate on 13 March 1912, "which was done better than any whale could do...."

Affiliation with an international union gave such local craftsmen a vivid sense of belonging to a much wider movement of workingmen, but the International was far less involved in the affairs of the Local than it had been in the nineteenth century or was to become after 1912. In 1901 and 1903 the International went along with the Local's strikes; only in 1910 does it appear that the International may have placed a damper on local militancy by requesting more information before sanctioning a strike. Organizers came and organizers went; they filled *The Carpenter* with useful details for the historian, but did not do much for the Halifax carpenters. The Local listened attentively on 20 August 1901 to "very interesting and appropriate remarks" by the AFL's Canadian point man, John Flett (who delivered a short address on "When I Was a Carpenter"), and in 1907 received Bro. W. J. Shields, noting with rather less enthusiasm that he "addressed the meeting at considerable length upon the work he had done in the maritime Provinces." Organizers also came to Halifax in 1908 and 1909. The talks delivered in 1908 by Pictou County native J.D. Cowper, general international organizer of the United Brotherhood, were typical in stressing the prestige carpenters would derive from belonging "to the largest body of skilled men ever brought together in the world"; most of his attention during his five-day tour was devoted to Halifax and the Western Counties of the province. Although institutional accounts tend to stress the activities of such organizers, it appears they played a minor supporting role — facilitating changes that were developing within the local working class rather than creating effective trade unionism out of thin air.

Local 83 was a loyal supporter of the international union. Although other Canadian carpenters, especially in Vancouver, urged the necessity of having a *national* board of directors in the International, Local 83 regarded such suggestions with suspicion (as suggested by the fact that the British Columbia request, raised first on 6 December 1904, was, like the earlier request to support women's suffrage, "laid over" and forgotten). It felt much more strongly the need for effective *regional* trade unionism, endorsing on 5 May 1903 a call from Local 943 of Sydney "for an organizing agent for the maritime Provinces." Local 83 voted to affiliate with the Trades and Labor Congress of Canada on 1 November 1901, and remained a supporter of the Congress throughout this period. It resolved to act on a request from P.M. Draper of the TLC in 1906 that it communicate with the executive of the United Brotherhood and ask them to affiliate and pay per capita tax on all their Canadian members. (Maritime locals—83 in Halifax, 1278 in Glace Bay and 1588 in Sydney—were reported to be strongly in favour of the Canadian locals affiliating with the TLC in balloting taken in 1907, and reported in the June 1907 *Carpenter*.) The Local sent Draper a donation in 1909 for the TLC campaign "to stop the tide of undesirable emigration to this Canada of ours."

Local 83 bore little resemblance to a contemporary craft union. It lacked the structural supports of the check-off (which had by this time achieved a hold in the coalfields) or the administration of written agreements. (The two arbitration awards of 1901 and 1903 were, it is true, landmarks in the evolution of written collective agreements in Nova Scotia, but neither left much in the way of administrative tasks in the hands of the union.) This craft union did not have a paid staff. Monies to those who performed services for the union were paid on an *ad hoc* basis. When Ira Mason presented the union with a $25 bill on 6 October 1903 for his services in negotiating the unpopular 1903 arbitration agreement, his request was laid on the table for three months and forgotten. Complex documents of the type Mason had helped negotiate were relatively recent;

until then negotiations with employers had been unsystematic, and the conduct of negotiating committees was questioned by restive members. The defeat in the strike of 1903 was caused at least partly by the union's lack of organization: there were no committees formed to perform specific strike functions, and the union's ability to discipline its own members was called severely into question.

The Local's relations with other trade unions were consistent with its craft orientation. It attempted to follow the American Federation of Labor's call to organize the unorganized and build central labour unions by organizing a building trades council, but the organizers of the council found the work "an uphill climb" and were ultimately unsuccessful. Local 83 rented its hall to other unions (among them the butcher workmen, electrical workers, the building labourers and the teamsters—although it complained of the disorderly way in which some of the labourers conducted their meetings), opened a subscription list in 1902 for Halifax's first labour newspaper, *The Toiler*, published in aid of locked-out printers, and voted support in 1905 for striking moulders at the Hillis Foundry. It responded to appeals from workers from further afield, especially although not exclusively in the Maritimes: to the fund-raising efforts of the Saint John Labor Council, and to the appeals for help from striking moulders in Moncton and Sackville. Perhaps most significantly, Local 83 helped organize other carpenters in the region. Halifax carpenters were instrumental in organizing the union in Truro. In the July 1903 issue of *The Carpenter,* the correspondent from Truro noted the union's success in winning a nine-hour day and an increase of 5¢ an hour, and observed, "Our success is certainly due to the organizing of our local union in November 1902 ... and to a great extent to the able assistance rendered us by Bro. Brooks of the Halifax Local. We finally won over all contractors but two, one of them a churchman who thought it consistent with his duty as a Christian to hold off and not sign our agreement." Even the first gavel of the Truro local was a gift from Halifax. Similar assistance was rendered to the carpenters in Amherst. The carpenters were much more hesitant in lending their support to the Halifax and District Trades and Labor Council, whose requests for money and alleged indifference to the affairs of the building trades led to debates within the Local. Like the carpenters, the council had drifted into a profound lethargy in 1906 and 1907, years in which, as President Ira Mason put it on 2 April 1907, "Unionism was at a very low ebb in Halifax." Disillusionment with the Labor Council fed on the council's distribution of the profits from Labour Day events and its inability to bring political pressure to bear against outside contractors; at the Local's meeting on 16 November 1909 the council was "raked ... from 'stem to stern' " and was said to have "grossly ignored" Local 83.

The carpenters widened their range of vision by contributing to the struggles of many other workers and by supporting, however reluctantly, the Labor Council. Yet one is struck by the overwhelming emphasis on aiding only those workers generally considered to be *skilled*. In marked contrast to British Columbia, for example, Halifax carpenters did nothing to aid the coal miners in their strikes to establish the United Mine Workers of America, even though they were fought, in part, on the question of the international unionism to which the craftsmen were strongly committed.[7]

Through most of these years Local 83 was a quiet outpost of respectable craft unionism, far removed in place and in spirit from the radical carpenters of the West. Many craftsmen loved the social life provided by the union. As Brother Harry Horne (born in 1875 and initiated 20 August 1907), recalled on 15 December 1959, at a ceremony in his honour, "In reflecting on past years he said he could remember the picnics the carpenters had over on McNab's Island and the big four horse teams they hired and filled with hay in the winter time for sleigh rides. With spirits high in one hand and a girl in the other he said they really enjoyed themselves." Old members of the union were remembered and honoured. Craft rituals, as in the nineteenth century, remained central to Lodge meetings. Just as in the nineteenth century, and especially before 1912, Labour Day provoked serious debates—over the colour of uniforms, whether gloves should be worn, how the regalia should be fitted out, whether the old or new banners should be carried. The Local's charter was draped for one month in black crepe to mark the death of any of its members. The more radical trade unionists of the early twentieth century ruthlessly mocked such practices as those of "coffin clubs," but for these craftsmen they were important fraternal traditions, whose roots lay far back in the nineteenth century.

Indeed, for many members, the strongest tie to the union was the fraternal one. Sick and house-bound members could count on a visit from friends in the union. Some were supported through a revived local benefit scheme. When a poor and distressed member was reported on 2 November 1909 as being unable to keep up with his dues, but could not be directly aided by the union because of constitutional provisions against loaning money to members, "... as the meeting was too small for a collection to be thought of, Bro Gatley in a spirit of brotherly love, quietly said he would advance the needful at once. It was accepted in the same spirit as offered, and the president remarking, Let brotherly love continue."

Many a craftsman's funeral was paid for through the union—either by the International, or by the Local raffling off the tool chests of deceased members. In an age of chronic insecurity, such benefits aroused strong emotions. When on 6 May 1912 the recording secretary noted the sums paid out by the international union to meet death and disability claims, he wrote emotionally, "Brothers, dwell well upon the latter figures, they mean more than tongue can tell, they have a history all of their own."

The institutional history of Local 83 so far appears to confirm the common impression that the craft unions clung with a tenacious conservatism to an old-fashioned approach no longer appropriate to a highly industrialized age. Local 83 did not, for instance, launch a massive organizing drive in the region's woodworking mills which could have safeguarded its partial achievement of the nine-hour day by extending it throughout the province, and was never tempted by the thought of abandoning craft principles of organization in favour of a more all-inclusive form of unionism. A precipitate enthusiasm for audacious novelties was never among Local 83's characteristic weaknesses.

Yet in other ways, Local 83, defending as best it could the craft legacy of the first period of its history, was passing through the opening phases of the second. It needed an immense effort of adaptation to adjust old ideas to new realities. This development is most visible in two fields: the local union's attitude towards employers and its political position.

Employers continued to be members of this union as late as 1912, but the union increasingly forced them to live up to its trade rules. (Brothers A.C. Collings and B.I. Walters asked the permission of Local 83 "to become employers of carpenter skill and would have none but union help" as late as 16 April 1912; permission was granted.) J.G. Colp, who was one of the most prominent employers in the nineteenth-century union, had 16 men working for him in 1901, and was one of the first to concede the demands of the strikers of that year. Colp was considered an honoured member of the union in the 1890s, and was frequently appeased. His position in the following decade was more difficult. On 18 August 1903, he claimed exemption from the payment of strike benefits and complained that his employees had been called out; two years later, on 16 May 1905, he was said to be paying below the union rate. He was evidently guilty of the same offence in 1910, for after the secretary was authorized on 17 May 1910 "to write Bro. Colp letting him know just where he stood, and for him to read, mark, learn and inwardly digest" the relevant sections of the constitution, he was charged with contempt, and finally told to sever his connection with Local 83.

Conflicts were reported with other employers within the union as well. Thomas Phalen, a union activist, charged on 5 July 1904 "that some Bosses, Members of the Union were trying to cut wages." These members were called in to answer further charges of hiring non-union men. Similarly, Bro. Allan, an employer in the union, was charged "in re working with non Union men, & Union men idle & discharged" on 16 June 1908. Employers may well have wished to retain their union membership because of the death and disability benefits, and many in the union doubtless hoped to advance to the ranks of the masters. But one is at the same time struck by the union's willingness to expel employers, even at the cost of losing union shops, if they did not play by the rules. This marked a shift from the nineteenth century.

Secondly, and more importantly, the union's political position changed. In contrast with Toronto and Hamilton, Halifax skilled workers of the nineteenth century created very little in the way of a coherent political presence, either on their own or within the two traditional parties. Now the city experienced, for the first time, a genuinely independent working-class political challenge. The carpenters, perhaps rather surprisingly, gave it strong support.

In many ways, the carpenters' turn to political action made sense on a pragmatic level. They had since the 1880s sought to persuade civic politicians to impose a tax on non-resident workers and made this the price of their qualified support for the municipal tax reforms desired by Halifax business. Given the new links emerging between business and the state in this period, carpenters had every reason to seek political influence at City Hall, whether over the ways in which the city fathers gave money to factories, paid for carpenter labour at the Exhibition, or awarded jobs. The carpenters would consider supporting candidates for civic office, but only with the understanding that such men would be committed to reforming the trade. When Mr. Clifford Harris, of the firm of W.T. Harris & Son, contractors, was mentioned as a candidate for the position of Alderman for working-class Ward 5, the union men were urged on 19 March 1912 to see to it that when approached by either Harris or his agents, "to give them to understand that everything possible would be done in his favour, and he on his part was to do all in his power to the consummation of the increase asked for on and after May 1/1912." The carpenters felt they were entitled to a just measure of civic patronage. After the union was informed by an alderman that an appointment of city carpenter it dearly wanted for one of its members was not going to be made, the secretary remarked on 2 March 1911, "It seems that, that small ruling body [the Board of Works] are going in for retrenchment and were starting with the poor man's job first." In 1911, the union presented a series of demands for the reform of the city, including a better deal for workingmen on city trams—to be backed up by a boycott if necessary.

From 1905 to 1912—years when craftsmen across the country were making a similar choice—Local 83 gradually aligned itself with the Halifax Labor Party.[8] Evidence of a broader range of political interests abounds. The union insisted on interviewing candidates for Mayor in

1905—none of whom were found satisfactory—and in subsequent years expressed its views on vaccination (unanimously opposed), sabbatarianism (enthusiastically supportive), and the Industrial Disputes Investigation Act (which on 8 January 1907—very early in the debate over federal industrial relations legislation—it "heartily condemned"). The union crossed a political threshold in 1909 when it endorsed the Labor Party candidacy of John Joy. The argument for the Labor Party could be tied closely to the traditional craft demands the carpenters had always put forward for protection in the labour market. As one union member put it, on 2 February 1909, "... by joining the Halifax Labor Party, and by contending with the different political parties on this same subject, we would, he thought, through the natural course of events be able in the near future to lead the Legislature and the City Council to frame a law or laws, whereby workmen coming in from [outlying] districts would be required to pay a tax before being allowed to work, as they have to do in other Cities, (say St. John for instance)." Those carpenters endorsing the Labor Party were well-established in the union, and the resolution which linked Local 83 to the Labor Party pledged the members to support and help finance its campaign. The union held a draw for the Labor Party and gave it at least $189.30. Carpenters attending meetings at the Carpenters' Hall were greeted with posters announcing the forthcoming Labor Party meeting featuring Keir Hardie, and with copies of that peculiar blend of moderate and Marxist journalism, the *Eastern Labor News*. The support of craftsmen for such campaigns across Canada was common, but never before in Halifax had some craftsmen and many unskilled labourers united on a political program.

A union which still contained employers—but endorsed the Labor Party; a union stubbornly adhering to decreasingly effective craft methods—but becoming increasingly class conscious: such were the contradictions found within the ranks of the carpenters on the eve of the First World War.

The recording secretary, James Rosborough, who came from an old family of Halifax carpenters and whose beautifully written minutes are such a rich treasure for the historian, spoke of these contradictions in his writing. One of the most telling examples of this crisis in the craft is a note he left concerning the funeral of one of Local 83's members. Funerals were a deeply rooted craft tradition. In the past, masters and journeymen would attend such events. Now, Rosborough noted, things were different. Although the deceased had been a man well-known in the craft and had worked for the same firm for 40 years, "not one member of that firm were men enough to spend a half hour of their valuable time at that grave side of our departed brother.... 'God help us all,' when we have such a class of employer to deal with. Just think and remember, a faithful employee for 40 years, more than a life time."

The old exclusivist strategies of craft were falling before the new vertically integrated employers; the old ideals of craft solidarity were crumbling before the blunt facts of class division. In the workplace, in the community, and even at the graveside, the old rules no longer held. But what new rules could take their place?

3

The New Unionism and Economic Crisis 1912-1926

I was down at the Builders Exchange with a delegation from our local union and some of the employers said that although they paid us at the rate of fifty-five cents an hour they had to figure our time at from eighty-five cents or a dollar or more if they could get it so you see we are not getting anything like what we create, and I think a great deal of this unrest to-day is brought about by the capitalist—the big employers. They are greedy. They are making a considerable profit but they still want more and I might say further that I truthfully think I have [travelled] in a good many cities in the north, south, east and west of Canada and I don't believe there is one city I have been in which is so expensive for workmen, and especially craftsmen, as it is in Halifax. We must have more money, and if we don't get it I will tell you straight there is going to be trouble. We have to live and it [doesn't] matter how poor we are we have the right to live and our families also have the right to live.... I don't want the silk dresses and fancy boots for my wife and children but I do want the things my labor produces at a price that will enable me to get them and I cannot get them with the condition things are in to-day and the time is coming when I will see my wife and children crying for food and what am I going to do[?]

— Joseph Gorman, a participant in the
Halifax building trades strike of 1919[1]

After over a decade of struggling to find a response to the new economic realities, Local 83 changed its strategy in 1912. It moved from relying on the exclusion of the unskilled to a strategy of attempting to organize most workers in carpentry and, in close alliance with other building trades unions, most workers in the construction industry.

This change in Local 83 was part of a continental pattern, as the United Brotherhood made a more serious effort to organize woodworking factories. The Halifax Local was directly reorganized in 1913 by Frank Duffy, the general secretary of the United Brotherhood of Carpenters and Joiners of America, ably assisted by the Brotherhood's general organizer, J.H. Potts. This was part of a regional pattern, too. Across the Maritimes, the local organizers of the Brotherhood launched councils of building trades unions, either within one trade (as in Cape Breton) or governing a variety of trades (as in Halifax).

The international union's contribution to this new attitude was substantial. Yet local leaders had to make the new policy succeed. This new generation of leaders had seen in their own work how hard it was to impose traditional craft methods on an industry being swept along in a fast current of social and economic change.

The rank-and-file workers were restless as well. A pre-war construction boom had swelled their ranks and intensified the demand for more effective organization. As the War proceeded, building trades workers fought the employers tenaciously. After its conclusion in 1918, and in the havoc of postwar Reconstruction, they participated fully in a wave of unrest in 1919 that brought not only a surge in militancy but a new emphasis on political power.

It was in the period 1912-1926 that carpenters and their craft were transformed.

The carpenters' strike of 1913 and the building trades strike of 1914 were the two major developments in Halifax which demonstrated that a new order had emerged. These strikes took place against a regional background of building trades militancy in the years just before the First World War.

In Saint John, carpenters and other building workers pushed for such changes as $3 for an eight-hour day (which was the demand of Saint John carpenters in 1911). Eight building strikes occurred in Saint John alone in the five-year period ending in 1913. In Cape Breton, strikers took on the woodworking factories. The District Council of the United Brotherhood of Carpenters and Joiners, made up of local unions in Sydney, New Waterford, and Glace Bay, fought for $3.30 and the nine-hour day for Sydney carpenters and woodworkers employed by Rhodes, Curry and Chappell Brothers, the largest woodworking firms in the area. R.R. Chappell, proprietor of a major woodworking factory, reflected that the strike against his company seemed to show a basic conflict over the principles of how the industry should work:

> There [appear] to be two [principles] involved in this strike; The nine
> hour day and the rate of wages, and while we cannot accept the nine
> hour day and compete with the factories and planing mills all over
> Nova Scotia and New Brunswick, that are working under more
> favorable conditions, and all with one or two exceptions, working ten
> hours and paying less wages than we are, we feel that the attempt of
> the Union to say what we shall pay is a dangerous thing to listen to as
> they have told us we must in the very near future pay all employees the
> same rate of wages and they further say that if we dismiss a man
> because we think he is not earning his wages, the Union will investi-
> gate and if, in their opinion, he should not have been dismissed, he
> must be taken back again. Hence the danger of losing all authority
> over employees if we allow the Union to have any say in the rating of
> our men.[2]

Although the strikers came out with a compromise reduction in hours
without a loss of pay, the very fact that some important branches of the
integrated construction companies were now organized and subject to
union controls was an event of great significance.

In Halifax, the carpenters' strike in 1913 and the smaller building trades
strike in 1914 unfolded in this context of protest in the construction
industry.

These strikes showed a new, far more combative style of craft unionism.
Offered a 2¢ raise without a strike by the Builders' Association in May
1912, Local 83 voted on 27 May to accept it, but the vote was split 37-17.
The membership of the union had risen by at least 50% in the previous
year, thanks in large part to the reorganizing efforts of the International.
Perhaps as a result, a major changing of the guard had taken place in
elections for the union executive in June, 1912; four positions out of seven
(including those of president and vice-president) changed hands.

Ralph Eisnor, who had joined Local 83 just one year earlier, became
president. He was a strong proponent of the Labor Party and of a more
militant style of trade unionism. On 21 March, 1913, Local 83 sent a
circular letter to the employers, noting the economic conditions which
would justify an increase for carpenters to 40¢ per hour on and after 1
April 1913. The employers, fearful of external competition, argued that
the demand was excessive: "At this rate," one contractor told the *Herald*
on 27 March, "the building business in this city would have to suspend."

But the carpenters believed they had right on their side. One of their
main arguments was that the cost of living was making it difficult for them
to support their families. In the *Echo* on 30 April, Jonathan Brooks, the
union's treasurer, produced careful estimates of the budget for his family
of six which showed that the annual earnings of $852.60 represented by
the rate of 35¢ per hour fell short of the minimum of $875.29 needed for
basic necessities.

After the union sent the employers its demands, the contractors replied in a letter of 24 March, 1913, which said they would increase the rate to 35¢ per hour, and that this was to be "the highest rate." The carpenters were outraged by this offer. Under the existing scale running from 32¢ to 40¢ many of them were already receiving over 35¢ per hour. These men now confronted a proposed wage cut.

On 1 April 1913, construction sites—including the Woodside Refinery, the Dennis Building, and the City Club—were quiet as 207 union men and (according to an invaluable book of strike minutes) between 60 and 70 non-union men quit work. A mass meeting at union headquarters in the Dispensary Building installed strike officers ("as has always been the custom") and nine sub-committees to handle dealings with the press, negotiating with the employer, supervising the room, and policing the waterfront and railway for the arrival of strikebreakers.

The 1913 strike showed a much more collective approach to bargaining. In 1889 and in 1901, the union had been willing to call off strikes on an employer-by-employer basis: when one contractor settled, his workers would return to work. Now Local 83 insisted that until a *general* agreement was reached, no member of the union should be allowed to work. Approached by individual contractors, the union replied on 1 April 1913 that "we are dealing with the Builders' Association and no men could go to work till a satisfactory Settlement was arrived at." In line with its new emphasis on unified bargaining in the trade, Local 83 insisted on a disciplined approach to employers, who were to be dealt with only *en bloc*.

The union was infused with a new spirit. Brothers were reported working at the Dennis Building, at the Drydock, at a cold storage facility on Argyle Street, at the Technical College, at the Dominion Coal Company's wharf, at the *Herald* building, at the Home of the Good Shepherd. They were all visited by the union, and those who continued working were picketed. The minutes on 9 April 1913 note that a record was to be kept "of all men working in defiance of the union and to be Posted to be dealt with after the strike." Of 207 members on strike, the names of 26 were crossed off, but only a few of these returned to work. Some, finding the strike pay of $4 per week a bit meagre, set out with the union's permission for the West or Boston, hoping to return when the strike was completed. The roll book and financial records of the strike suggest that the carpenters held remarkably firm: 192 men claimed the first strike pay on 21 April; 205, the second on 28 April; 201, the third on 5 May; and 182, the fourth on 12 May. The union claimed in the *Acadian Recorder* of 10 April that it had enrolled at least 30 new members in the first two weeks of the strike. In vivid contrast with the strike of 1903, the Local was able to discipline its members and increase its numbers.

Even more impressive was the carpenters' aggressive response to the problem of protection from outside labour. Sentinels were posted at the Railway Station, Three Mile House Road, the North West Arm, and on the Waterfront to watch for outside workers. Their short reports from 2 to 26 April speak vividly of a craft under siege:

> *Report from Railway Committee saw a man Bro. Worth from New Glasgow, he did not know about the trouble and reported in Afternoon at Meeting.
>
> *Reported by Piquets no suspicious characters were seen in City. Railway Piquets reported Favourable seeing nobody looking like a carpenter.
>
> *Piquet on Railway reported 4 men came in—who went to work on the construction company Job—that a Poster was pasted on one man's Tool Box—Carpenters Stay away from Halifax.
>
> *Yates Reported Garrison left the City—also Brookfield Ltd. got agents out [to recruit strikebreakers] and Falconer & Macdonald also—up to us to get Busy—Canvass on the trains. But it was shown it was against the rules.... Bro Yates Chairman of Railway Com. to have a free hand to give material assistance to those he was dealing with in the matter of train tickets etc.
>
> *Bro. Brooks reported seeing a man a Stranger from Outside the City after some conversation found he was going to work on the Construction Company's job.
>
> *Bro. Crowe captured Two men persuading them not to go to work and secured a boarding Place for them, till they left the City.
>
> *The President stated that the [vessel] Numidian was due today or tonight urging the Piquet to keep a Bright look out as it was reported a number of carpenters were coming on Her.
>
> *Another man came in to work for a Doctor who when aware of trouble stated he would sooner sleep in the Bush than work while carpenters were on Strike.
>
> *Bro. Gray reported the emigrant agents giving them every assistance to capture carpenters coming in by Steamers and more had come in by last Steamer.
>
> *Bro. Yates reported a Tool Box at station from the Western Shore— came by train.

Capturing carpenters, scanning the railway stations for the tell-tale boxes of carpenters' tools, sending pickets to control the influx of strikebreakers: the tactics of Local 83 in 1913 show how far the union had come from the world of the nineteenth century.

This strike would be won or lost, both sides realized, through control over the labour market. Advertisements in the *Chronicle* (on 18 April) and the *Echo* (21 April and 7 May) from the Nova Scotia Construction Company, Limited, invited carpenters to apply for work at its offices. The union responded vigorously to this challenge. On 1 May, when a significant body of men did get through the carpenters' defenses to work at the Dartmouth refinery, the union dispatched "a Strong com[mittee of] 20 men" to go down to the job site. At least one contractor threatened to lay charges because "men working at his Premises had been badly threatened by union men." Local 83's President cautioned the men to avoid milling in a threatening crowd outside the Board of Trade Rooms.

The critical area to control was rural Nova Scotia. Posters advertising the strike were sent to Milton, Liverpool, Port Medway, Brooklyn, Shelburne, Yarmouth and New Germany, with instructions to postmasters to put them up. As many as 500 strike posters were sent through the country, while the union gathered intelligence on potential movements of strikebreakers from Sydney, Fredericton, Liverpool and Yarmouth.

As the two sides countered each other's moves in the labour market, James Rosborough of the carpenters and H.S. Freeman of the Exchange traded letters. What these letters (published in the *Acadian Recorder* of 9 and 12 April) reveal is an insistence on the part of the union that employers form a coherent body with which they could bargain.

On 4 April Freeman told Rosborough the carpenters had misconstrued the employers' position; he now claimed that a 3¢ raise was being offered to those rated as foremen and getting 35¢ per hour. "While I am sorry you misunderstood me," he wrote, "I cannot see why an explanation was not asked [for] instead of ending our negotiations in such a summary manner." Rosborough replied the next day. "Our letter to you of April 1st we thought clearly stipulated that negotiations be opened up between your Association and the Union, but up to date no word has been received from you other than that of April 4th, which the meeting assembled cannot quite understand." Was Freeman speaking for the builders or for himself? On 8 April a letter from Freeman (which the minutes record was "read and *dissected*") told the carpenters their strike was improper: "We hold that you broke off negotiations when you went out on strike without notice, which is contrary 1st, to your agreement with us; 2nd, to all business principles; 3rd, to the rules of your own Union." On 8 April the union again requested that the builders appoint a committee to meet a like committee from the men to dispose of the question at issue, and in a release to the press disputed Freeman's contention that any agreement was still in force between the Master Builders' Association and the Carpenters' Union. When the carpenters finally did meet a committee from the employers on 9 April, they were told that the committee "had no Power to settle anything in connection with the present trouble—But just met them to know what the Carpenters wanted...."

To make matters yet more complicated, the Builders' Association then assumed that this committee had made an offer of 3¢, an offer the carpenters denied ever receiving. In the pages of the *Echo* of 24 April, the Association said it would permit this offer to stand until 1 May, and then withdraw it. When this deadline passed, the Association noted provocatively in the *Herald* of 5 May 1913 that "a number of carpenters are available, and new men are arriving daily." The carpenters then pursued with other building trades unions the idea of conducting a general building strike, and made arrangements to set up their own workshop.

The strike was finally settled with a 3¢ increase, which raised the minimum rate from 32¢ to 35¢, and applied to all higher rates as well. Although it fell short of the carpenters' original demand by leaving employers with the discretion to pay journeymen within a range of wages lower than those the carpenters had wanted, it was still a more satisfactory deal than had been first offered by the Builders' Association. The failure of the other building trades unions to support the carpenters in 1913 was the critical turning point: had they come out on strike, the building season and the contracts waiting the completion of the strike would have been forcibly held up.

Both sides crossed a Rubicon with this strike. In its aftermath both took steps to organize more effectively. The employers strengthened their resolve to resist trade unionism. They created the Constructive Mechanical Trades Exchange, which trade union organizers told the *Herald* on 27 June 1914 was incorporated with "a determination to fight trades unionism." And labour created Halifax's first effective Building Trades Council, to unite building workers in the various crafts.

The first critical test of the Building Trades Council came at the new science building at Dalhousie University in May, 1914, when construction workers quit work claiming that non-union plumbers were being employed by the sub-contractors. (Some 15 or 20 carpenters were involved, employees of Falconer and McDonald, the contractors.) This was the first twentieth-century "sympathetic" strike in the history of the Halifax building trades. Labour returned to work in late May, evidently on favourable terms.

Some contractors were alarmed by the strength of the building trades' new organization which was revealed in this strike. F.D. Pierce, the secretary of this new Building Trades Council, tried to soothe worried contractors in an interview with the *Chronicle* on 13 May. He argued "that the Building Trades Council is not an organization formed for the purpose of stirring up trouble or of holding up employers for more wages by means of a general strike or anything of this kind. On the contrary one of its chief aims is to promote a feeling of harmony between employee and employer, and if possible, to settle all disputes by peaceful means on a basis fair to both parties." He reported that the "aggressive campaign mapped out by the Council in the early months of the year" was already beginning to show gratifying results "in increased membership in every union affiliated."

But employers were neither soothed nor gratified by Pierce's rhetoric. Instead, they were outraged by a letter from Pierce to their Association, which said, in its entirety, "I have been instructed by the Halifax Building Trades Council to inform you that on and after May 1, 1914, no union man in the following trades—carpenters, painters, plumbers, electrical workers, steamfitters or plasterers—will work on any job unless all workmen in those trades working on the job are furnished with building trades cards for the then current quarter. This applies to Halifax and vicinity." According to the *Herald* of 15 May, once they had listened to that letter, the employers moved that their Association "will unanimously stand for the open shop, in view of the fact that in their opinion the action of the Trades Council is in the line of coercion."

To enforce discipline within their own ranks, the employers threatened in July 1914 to boycott master plumbers who acceded to the demands of labour. The Building Trades Council and the employers went to battle on the question of labour rights in the columns of the daily press in August, 1914. The plumbers' strike affected all the other building trades, because, as the *Herald* of 28 July noted, "No man is going to start building a house if he is aware of the fact that the plumbers are not going to work on it." On 30 June 1914, at a mass meeting of 500 men from all of the building trades, the employers were threatened with a general strike of all the allied unions in the building trades in sympathy with a plumbers' strike for increased wages, and in protest against the Exchange's importation of strikebreakers. The employers refused to consider arbitration because, they told the *Acadian Recorder* on 23 July, "the local government invariably favored the workingmen." Under the threat of a general building trades strike, however, the dispute went to arbitration and a compromise was effected.[3]

On the eve of the First World War, capital and labour in the building trades were polarized as they had never been before. The 1913 strike was an especially significant stage in this process, because it marked a new level of militancy and a significant broadening of perspective on the part of Local 83. Support for the carpenters and other building workers was aroused in the public as well. The *Dartmouth Patriot* condemned the employers in an editorial on 17 May, remarking, "This few took the lordly, high and mighty stand that they were the absolute arbiters not only of their own affairs but also of [those] of their fellows, their employees who forsooth, must slave-like accept whatever rate they saw fit to name.... The time has long since passed for the assumption of any such arrogance in dealing with any respectable body of men, in matters of this kind."

Wayne Roberts says of Toronto carpenters during these years that they "had seen their traditional craft methods crumble, unable to control the labour pool or restrain employers. To overcome these weaknesses, they had to overcome the past." While some craftsmen within woodworking were able to preserve their sense of being highly skilled artisans, the carpenters were transformed into "modern wage-workers, totally alienated from their skill and workmanship. On the one hand we have respectable citizens; on the other outcasts."[4]

The Halifax situation was possibly a bit less dramatic. In 1913 carpenters did not behave like outcasts; they behaved like aggrieved, but very respectable, citizens, forced to resort to a strike to protect themselves. Craft rituals had not declined, and the support for the Halifax Labor Party did not mean support for revolution. But Roberts captures the general truth of their position. Halifax carpenters were forced to rethink their craft ideology, their stance towards other workers, and their positions within the "trade"—all along the lines of class. The carpenters had completed their long training in the art of survival in the new economy. Their postwar radicalism, while greatly intensified by the catastrophes of war, came out of this decades-long apprenticeship.

Halifax, more than any other Canadian city, was reshaped by the First World War. The population swelled to meet the demands of war production. A severe housing shortage caused rents to increase dramatically. Then came the massive Explosion on 6 December 1917, which destroyed over one square mile of the working-class North End and killed (according to low official estimates) 1,963 people. Halifax was forced to take postwar "reconstruction" far more literally than any other North American city.

Even before the war, and in part because of the redevelopment of the port and naval facilities, Halifax's construction industry had grown more rapidly than the industry nationally. Building permits (as recorded by the *Labour Gazette*) posted a 173% increase—from $484,040 to $879,320 from 1910 to 1914 inclusive. (In contrast, the national tables, based on 35 major Canadian cities, indicated a 4% drop in permits.)

Many buildings of Dalhousie University, the city market, a new immigration shed on Pier 2, and the new Deep Water terminals kept local building workers active. The War did not entail an immediate change in the level of construction in the city. In January 1915, for example, the *Labour Gazette* reported that the industry had entered its seasonal slump, with only two institutional contracts of any consequence still being pushed ahead, and all building trades connected with the Halifax and District Trades and Labor Council reported a slackening of work and a good deal of unemployment.

But in sharp contrast with the national pattern, Halifax did not experience a drop in the value of new construction. Across the 35 cities surveyed by the Department of Labour, there was a sharp decline in the value of building permits from 1914 to 1916; 1916 building permits in Halifax, however, were 39% higher than the level in 1914. In 1917, building tradesmen worked on renovations to the new hospital for returned soldiers, the new Imperial Oil Company plant, and new terminal piers.

The explosion of 1917 set off a boom of a different sort in 1918.

After slackening slightly in 1917, the Halifax building industry posted an extraordinary advance to $2,866,852 in building permits, a 342% rise from 1913 without taking inflation into account, and an estimated 169% on the basis of a 50.5% inflationary increase in the average weighted wholesale prices of building materials. In 1918, the *Labour Gazette* revealed, only Toronto and Montreal exceeded the Halifax total. It was a sudden bonanza.

With Rev. L.J. Donaldson, who gave a curious speech on the "Brighter Aspects of the Catastrophe" in January, 1918, the contractors of Halifax could look forward to increased material prosperity through the expenditure of millions of dollars in one of the largest construction projects in Nova Scotian history. In 1919, new building permits worth a remarkable $5,194,805 were issued in Halifax.

Reconstruction meant the importation of thousands of new workers and a feverish pace of production. Local sash, door and planing mills worked day and night, and even in distant Ottawa such mills were kept busy making materials for Halifax. "Never were the painters and decorators of this city rushed with work as they are today," enthused a blurb for the Halifax Painting and Decorating Company Limited in the *Herald* on 19 August 1918, "and when one considers the thousands of houses that were badly wrecked by the explosion and that after seven months of steady work only a very small proportion of them have been repaired and re-decorated, the immensity of the task becomes apparent, and the success of a firm able to handle the work seems assured." Contractors and workingmen alike flocked to the city, attracted by the the *Labour Gazette*'s description of "plenty of employment for all classes of workers, skilled and unskilled." As the Census reveals, from 1911 to 1921, the number of builders and contractors rose from 60 to 387, while total employment in the industry went from 1,263 to 2,384 persons. These statistics understate the case, because they capture the situation only after the huge boom in construction had passed its peak.

Construction workers were at the heart of regional labour unrest during the War. Employers committed to the open shop confronted workers now far less restrained by the craft tradition. In Saint John in 1917, master plumbers claimed to be enjoying "the most profitable business period they have experienced in many years" after they managed to do the work of striking journeymen. The bitter reaction to this complacent dismissal of trade-union rights could be found in the arrests of plumbers for intimidation, arson and murder during a tragic strike.

It was an extreme example of a more general regional phenomenon. The situation in Halifax was somewhat less charged, perhaps, but no less polarized. When electrical workers went on strike in 1917, notwithstanding a contract which was to hold good until 1918, a contractor bitterly compared them in the *Herald* of 11 July to the enemies Canadian boys were fighting in Europe. "They have shown about as much respect for that contract as did the Germans for their 'scrap of paper'.... They have evidently determined to take advantage of the present lack of men." The workers replied, "The contractors seem to infer that we are taking advantage of the lack of men, but have also forgotten to mention the fact that we have carried on negotiations for weeks and failing to come to a reasonable settlement, they have not hesitated to precipitate this trouble by discharging their men, en bloc, thus not taking advantage of a time limit, in which a settlement might have been arrived at, if the employers had shown any willingness of being fair."

The electrical contractors had brought in workers from across the country, but resented the trade-union traditions many such workers brought with them. "We resent the coming to the city of a French Canadian to make trouble for local firms," one contractor remarked. "We were conducting negotiations with our own men, which promised to result harmoniously and satisfactorily when Mr. Beaulieu arrived ... and there was an immediate change."

While the War was on, workers were often persuaded to defer their demands until the battle was over; with its end, they had a long list of grievances. They had watched contractors do very well out of the War, and (as can be seen from the words of Joseph Gorman which begin this chapter) they bitterly criticized the employers' greed. Building craftsmen wanted to replace their chaotic conditions of employment with greater security and power. To do so, they had to meet three related challenges.

The first was controlling the new labour market. New workers arrived by the thousands. In January 1918, 3,200 workers were directly engaged under the Reconstruction Committee; according to remarks of J.C. Harris published in the *Herald* on 27 March 1919, as many as 6,000 tradesmen arrived in the city in 1918 and 1919.

Local 83's membership rose steeply, according to the membership rolls, from 204 and 215 members in 1915 and 1917 respectively, to 469 members in 1918 and 1,270 members at the end of 1919. The union was reported to be "1100 strong" in the Halifax *Citizen* on 20 June 1919.

Many workers faced the special difficulties of migrants adjusting to a different city. Painters hired for the Reconstruction effort, for example, were mainly from Montreal. "I belong to Montreal," Joseph Gorman told the Royal Commission on Industrial Relations in 1919, "and I have been away from my wife and family since July [11 months] and I have made every effort to maintain them, and I have felt that it was my right as a workman if I was unable to sell my labor in one city I shall be permitted to take my labor to another city where I can dispose of it, because I am absolutely dependent upon my labor and upon my labor alone for my bread and butter." He had left Montreal for Halifax after he had "tramped the city from one [end] to the other unable to find employment."[5] Local 83's membership rolls suggest a large influx of carpenters from Western Nova Scotia and the Gaspé as well as Montreal. Living in substandard and costly housing, and faced with a soaring cost of living, these new workers were impatient for improvements in their condition and frequently became staunch trade unionists.

The leadership of the labour movement had changed as dramatically as its rank and file. Most of the local building unions (including Local 83) retained their pre-war leadership. But the cause of the American Federation of Labor, with which they were affiliated, was being championed in Halifax by the dynamic C.C. Dane, an Australian. Dane mobilized workers from one end of the province to the other, from Amherst to Sydney. While he represented the AFL, he was a far cry from the tradition of Samuel Gompers. Craft unionism in his hands became mass unionism with a radical edge. "I am a Bolshevist," he told the Industrial Relations Commission in 1919, "and I will warn these two Governments that trouble is coming and the men will have what belongs to them."[6] Dane helped keep the AFL dominant in the Maritimes by absorbing the radical energies which might otherwise have taken regional workers in other directions.

The second challenge before Halifax building craftsmen was to preserve some control over the thousands of building sites in Halifax. Electrical workers were up in arms in 1917 over the employment of apprentices to do work which, under the law, was only supposed to be done by licensed workers. They appealed for redress from City Council. As noted in the *Herald* on 8 May 1920, the Building Trades Council—now a powerful body—pressed the City Council to enforce a clause in the city charter covering workers in the trades employed on city contracts, noting that during the spring and summer months "there was a considerable influx of outside workers into the city whose pay was much lower than the schedule of wages."

This defence of craft rights was particularly difficult in the wake of the Halifax Explosion. Local 56 of the United Association of Plumbers and Steamfitters, in particular, was the focus of much venomous criticism for its devotion to craft principles. The trade union did not endear itself to the *Herald* when it protested to the Board of Health over the bringing in of outsiders and alleged that such outside workmen were destroying considerable amounts of plumbing material through lack of skill. The *Herald* condemned on 18 January 1918 "The Heartless Attitude and Cold-Blooded Indifference of the Plumbers' Union of Halifax," which, it charged, had declined to lift a finger to help stricken fellow citizens and refused aid to the "Homeless and Suffering in Body and Mind, in the Bitterest Winter Within the Memory of Man." Through their president, "the plumbers have declined, point blank, to waive one jot or title from their iron-clad 'regulations' demanding those extra rates for overtime.... The plumbers of Halifax thus violate the commonest dictates of humanity to stricken fellow beings." It was equally shrill in its attitude to bricklayers, who refused to allow the plasterers to help in the repair of chimneys.

These points made by the *Herald* and other commentators were a trifle cheap. Halifax craftsmen (many of whom had suffered bitterly from the Explosion themselves) were being asked to give up time-honoured achievements of hours restriction and traditions of craft demarcation, but contractors were required to give up neither their power nor their profits. As Ralph Eisnor of Local 83 and the Labor Council explained to the Relief Commission, "We have worked thirty or thirty-five years to complete our organization and to get what we have got, and while we regret the calamity which has befallen our City, we cannot see any reason why people are coming in and running slipshod over all our trade regulations.... We were quite willing to overlook any discrepancy of that kind in the first stages of the work.... Our grievance is that we do not want men coming in here and our trade rules and regulations run over."[7]

So seriously did labour take this question that national trade-union leaders were brought in to intervene before the Commission.[8] The Halifax Relief Commission did come to an understanding with the plumbers; the union agreed to waive overtime pay for work of "urgent rehabilitation" until 1 May, "with the distinct understanding that this action would not be used as a precedent to break down established conditions." The Halifax plasterers in February of 1918 had asked for an increase of 10¢. The Reconstruction Commission requested that the demand be deferred until 1 May. The craftsmen agreed to defer their demands, and the *Herald* reported that many worked as long as thirteen hours per day repairing the houses in the city "with huge rents in the ceilings and wall where the plaster fell" in the Explosion. Only after some months had passed did the plasterers go on a short strike to enforce their demand for payment from the Reconstruction Commission on the same basis as all the other union plasterers in the city. Although organized labour was very upset that non-unionists were hired on such projects as the massive Hydro-Stone development—only 60% of the workers in such trades as the carpenters, painters, plumbers and labourers were unionized—it did not strike to enforce the closed shop.[9]

Such temporary concessions should not, the craftsmen felt, be transformed into permanent defeats. The generally anti-labour Commission did little to put pressure on prospering contractors to make Reconstruction fair to the workers.

The third challenge was the maintenance of living standards in a time of high inflation. The acute inflationary pressures of this period are well known. They were aggravated in Halifax by an extreme shortage of working-class housing and the apparent profiteering of some merchants. The cost of living was cited by everyone who spoke on the new militancy of the building trades after the War. "Some people may say that these men are asking for extortionate rates per hour," remarked the *Citizen* on 9 May 1919, but the individual carpenter was merely trying to keep pace with inflation: "Five years ago when he was receiving 40 cents an hour he was paying $6.00 a barrel for flour—now he is paying $12.00—a 100 per cent increase...."

"The time is coming when I will see my wife and children and crying for food and what am I going to do?" Joseph Gorman had asked the Commission on Industrial Relations. A lot of building craftsmen were asking that question in 1919. It seemed only a massive struggle would enable them to preserve wartime gains. For contractors in early 1919, the building prospects appeared bright with a number of larger contracts in sight—the extension of the Bank of Nova Scotia building from Hollis to Granville Streets; the new building for the Imperial Tobacco Company; the Navy League building; a new tuberculosis hospital near Fairview; and scores of dwelling houses. But for workers the postwar period was one of dislocation and unrest. There was an atmosphere of urgency, even desperation, as the building crafts met with contractors in early 1919.

Workers in 1919 mounted the largest and most serious labour revolt in Canadian labour history. As historian Gregory S. Kealey has observed, the 1919 revolt represented a return to the pre-war pattern of conflict, but at a higher level of intensity.[10]

The building crafts have generally been ignored, for the understandable reason that compared with the Winnipeg General Strike, smaller building trades disputes in Halifax, Kingston, and Ottawa faded into the background. But without trying to present the Halifax Building Trades Strike of 1919 as the Winnipeg Strike it clearly never was, one can still say that it was a strike which raised radical questions and was carried out, at least until its conclusion, in a radical manner. In 1919 it represented the biggest strike yet in the history of Halifax. Sparked by immediate pressures (the high cost of living, miserable housing conditions, and so on), the 1919 strike was possible only as the climax of a very protracted process of class polarization. Never before, and rarely since, have Halifax building craftsmen had a united militancy like that of 1919.

"There is considerable building going on in Halifax," wrote a worried commentator for the *Herald* on 26 April 1919, "but at the same time there is depression. This is due to two causes—the difficulty in obtaining material and its cost and the unrest in labor circles.... The men claim that living is higher [than] in many other cities, notably in the excessive charges for rent. The employers say the pay demanded when compared with that obtaining in other cities is an impossibility. In reference to the scarcity of houses, it is urged that this is temporary and that the situation is being relieved by accommodation that has been provided in the devastated area for about 250 families." Local 83 opened the 1919 campaign in March by writing to employers that the rate for carpenters was to be 75¢ an hour. By April, nine building trades unions—representing carpenters, plumbers, steamfitters, masons, plasterers, bricklayers, stone cutters, electrical workers and painters—demanded the same increase, and the eight-hour day, effective 1 May, 1919.

These remarkable 1919 wage demands marked a new unified state in the history of the building craftsmen. Until 1919, only in rare cases in which building craftsmen felt a contractor was violating an important trade rule had "sympathetic" strikes occurred involving several building trades at once. Craftsmen had negotiated separately and by 1919 wide gaps had emerged, for example, between the high rates commanded by electricians and the low wages of painters. But now craftsmen, by demanding the same rates for all the trades and by bargaining together, were transforming craft unionism into something more like industrial unionism. (Significantly, however, a line was drawn between the craftsmen and the building labourers.) It was the "Amalgamated Trades Union" of the nineteenth century reborn in a different age.

The employers sensed the challenge presented by this new style of craft unionism. They first responded by suggesting a new system of grading carpenters into first-class, second-class, and third-class men, all to be paid according to ability. They then counter-offered in a way which redivided the crafts along lines of skill, offering a 10% increase to most, but less to the carpenters (whose rate was to be placed at 63¢ per hour). "One reason why the carpenters are offered less than the other trades," a spokesman for the employers told the *Herald* on 28 April 1919, "is that with them no stated terms of apprenticeship are required as in the case of the men in their co-unions. In this respect many of the carpenters are classed as less 'skilled' than is the case with men in unions where learners must serve time or where an examination is demanded before work is permitted."

As the strike proceeded, both labour and capital tested the unity of the opposing camp and attempted to make the most of any division in the ranks. The strategy of divide-and-rule worked for the employers to a limited extent. Two unions out of nine (the stone cutters, who settled for the old rate after a short strike in early April, and the sheet metal workers, who accepted the 10% offer in mid-May) made peace with the Exchange.

But the other unions held firm. At a meeting on 30 April, Local 83, made up of about 800 carpenters, voted unanimously for the strike. When the strike commenced on 1 May, with an estimated 1,500 participants, hundreds of non-unionists joined the striking unions. "A considerable number of non-union men remained at work," noted the *Herald* on 3 May 1919, "but these are a comparatively small proportion when compared with the union strikers." By 8 May 1919 the Halifax *Citizen*, a labour paper strongly supported by Local 83, reported organizer Hedley Marks's estimate that Local 83 had grown from 800 to 1,300 members in one week.

Not only were contractors frustrated in their efforts to create a significant division in labour's ranks, but they soon discovered that divide-and-rule cut both ways. Three electrical contractors signed agreements with their workers at the advanced wage, pending a settlement of the general question. L.J. Dorey, business agent for the plasterers, noted that not quite 10% of his union's membership was employed by members of the Exchange. On 10 May he advised the *Herald* that over half of his members were working under agreement, but 25% were still on strike because of the pressure brought to bear on smaller contractors by the Exchange, "which forbids the smaller boss to adhere to our agreement and threatens to hold the work from them." The *Citizen* of 30 May remarked explicitly on the carpenters' strategy. "In the field of defense the carpenters take as their motto, 'in union there is strength.' For the offensive they say 'divide and conquer.' Accordingly they are permitting some employers to have men who sign the union scale." According to the same source, about 20% of the carpenters had been placed at the advanced rate demanded by labour as of 6 June.

The carpenters' spokesmen returned time and again to the differences between the large and small contractors. John T. McGrath, business agent for Local 83, commented in the *Citizen* on 6 June, "The little fellows haven't had half a dozen war years behind them, and haven't the same standing with the banks; so when they see the summer [slipping] away with all chance of making money disappearing, they naturally want to get out from under."

According to reports in both the labour and mainstream press, the strike was conducted with remarkable order and discipline. One reason for this was the generous financial support given the strike by the international unions: the carpenters received $15,000 from their headquarters in the first week of June. (The United Brotherhood allotted this strike $25,000.) No more than 50 out of 1,100 striking carpenters deserted the strike, despite tempting offers from the contractor of the Roy Building that anyone working with him would receive the advance offered by the employers. The most disorderly aspect of the strike was an argument between the carpenters and painters during a baseball game on the South Common. The Montreal *Star* worried that given the recent riots in Halifax, the large building trades strike might easily set off serious disturbances, and one eminent judge urged the Exchange to bring the case under federal industrial relations legislation in the interests of social peace. However, such fears of mass disturbance proved groundless.

Yet it could easily have been otherwise, especially had the employers succeeded in recruiting the army of strikebreakers they were trying to raise in Montreal. Had a member of the Exchange re-opened with non-union labour, or had the police broken up the crowds of men on the streets, the strike might have overflowed the banks of AFL craft unionism.

In the third week of June, according to the *Citizen* of 23 June 1919, the Halifax trade unions voted in a referendum on the holding of a general city-wide strike, perhaps as a way of forcing employers to the bargaining table. It was probably no accident that shortly after the vote was held the Constructive Mechanical Trades Exchange abandoned its attempts to enforce the open shop through the recruitment of strikebreakers in Montreal and agreed to bargain collectively with the unions.

One of the workers' central demands was for "collective bargaining," but by this they meant something far different from the orderly process of negotiation which we normally associate with this term. Collective bargaining in 1919 meant a step away from craft unionism towards bargaining involving much larger and more powerful units. The demand for collective bargaining had a distinctly radical edge. The *Herald* on 6 June captured the spirit of the times, and this more radical sense of the term, when it commented that while some strikes might be justified, this "must not be regarded as justification for what are known as 'sympathetic strikes,' much less strikes for an untried theory such as 'collective bargaining' and 'one big union.' Such movements are symptomatic of social disease; they are subversive of democratic institutions; they are, in short, revolutionary...."

When the Exchange offered in early June to confer with one arbitrator representing all the striking unions, this was seen as the triumph of collective bargaining. The *Citizen* on 6 June saw it as "recognition of the essential solidarity of labor, whatever the craft...." Yet the offer was considered very cautiously by the unions. "The reason the carpenters and some others take this attitude is that they feel they may be betrayed if they go back to work and help the contractors to clean up on their contracts, as the latter will then be in a position to stave off a decision until they are out of a hole," noted the *Citizen*. "If the men keep away from the job, the bosses are sure to be interested and anxious for a quick decision."

The arbitration of the dispute took place under provincial arbitration legislation. It was considered "a unique feature in labor history" that the trade unions should choose an employer, J.A. McDonald, the president of Amherst Pianos, Limited, as their representative on the board. The unions' choice of McDonald was less quixotic than it first appeared; he was known to have been favourable to labour's side in previous hearings, and he was later to win accolades for his settlement of the dispute in Moncton between building craftsmen and contractors working on the T. Eaton Co. building.

The proceedings were a triumph of quiet diplomacy. One side would present its case in writing, and this was then placed in the hands of the other side, which had 24 hours to prepare its rebuttal, and then both submissions were considered by the arbitrators. "During all the meetings there was not an unkind or a disrespectful word uttered on either side," the arbitrators noted in handing down their award.

The *Citizen* on 27 June said there was "a general air of suppressed jubilation" when the arbitration decision was announced to the various crafts. The arbitrators gave masons, bricklayers, and plasterers the 75¢ per hour rate they had demanded, the electricians and plumbers 70¢ and the carpenters and painters 66¢. The wage increases ranged from 32% for the carpenters to 17% for the electricians. However, the award also represented the craft status quo in that it reimposed the differentials between the various crafts and urged "the different unions to take steps for the proper classification of workmen," without which the higher interests of the "best workmen" could never be secured.

It was a rather anti-climactic end to a long strike. For the *Herald*, which ran an editorial on the subject on 6 June, the Halifax strike showed just how sensible local labour was in contrast with the wild westerners. "Organized labor in Nova Scotia has at nearly all times been well-led and reasonable," the *Herald* argued. "It is maintaining its traditions in these present times of wild talk and dangerous proceedings." Looking askance at the general strike in the West, the *Herald* remarked, "There is no danger of anarchy in this province."

But the *Chronicle*'s editor drew a different conclusion. First he looked at Winnipeg, which dramatized the futility of revolutionary politics, and then turned to Halifax. "The Halifax strike also had its lessons, scarcely less important," he argued. "For nearly two months at the most important season of the year, when public need was the greatest, building operations were brought to a standstill in this city. It was worse than misfortune. It was a calamity for all concerned, the effects of which will be bitterly felt by innocent sufferers hereafter."

What conclusions should be reached about the Great Building Trades Strike of 1919?

It was remarkable, given their past history, that the Halifax craft unions had brought the city to the very edge of a General Strike and listened to a radical such as C.C. Dane. But it is also plain that the craft unions were able to survive 1919 by absorbing small doses of radicalism and syndicalism without really changing in their nature. The award helped to confirm this ambiguous result.

In one way the outcome of the 1919 strike was a victory for the building trades, and confirmed that "collective bargaining" could get results. In another way, however, the opposite was true. Whatever unity building craftsmen may have glimpsed in 1919 was quickly eroded by the award and by the reversion to normal craft unionism in the 1920s. Craft barriers, which were frequently breached in the postwar wave of enthusiasm for the AFL in the east, were quietly re-erected; the Building Trades Council slowly disintegrated; and only after decades did craftsmen unite again for a general building strike quite different than that of 1919. Most importantly, the award meant the various crafts were paid at very different rates, and these rates would diverge more and more from each other as time went on. Although the building trades strike represented a major challenge to traditional craft unionism, it also indicated that such a challenge could be contained within the established union structures.

Just as the strike of 1919 marked the ambivalent climax of a long process of class division in the industry—ambivalent because it marched craftsmen outside the barriers of craft and then marched them back again—the development of postwar progressive politics in the building trades brought the carpenters' pre-war political interests to a new level, but ultimately suggested the fragility of craft "radicalism."

The carpenters, perhaps more than any other labour group in Halifax apart from the shipyard workers, identified themselves with radical politics after the First World War. The revitalized Halifax Labor Party—after the War part of the powerful province-wide Farmer-Labor movement—was officially reborn in the Carpenters' Hall at a special meeting of the Trades and Labor Council on 23 July 1919.[11] The president of the Council and the head of Local 83, Ralph Eisnor, chaired the meeting. Eisnor had intended to run as a labour candidate in the 1917 election but, because of the Explosion, he retired from the field and the election went by acclamation. He was a vice-president of the Trades and Labor Congress of Canada and by common consent the pre-eminent labour leader in the city. His address called upon Halifax workingmen to take part in the "onward march of the proletariat." Joe Wallace, who had achieved a reputation for radical activism in his work with the Halifax *Citizen*, joined with Eisnor in calling for a party similar to the British Labour Party.

In 1919 Local 83 was an important centre for radical agitation in the city, and it remained one long after hopes for immediate victory had faded. In 1920, Local 83 supported the Halifax *Citizen* morally and financially and generously gave $200 to the Halifax Labor Party. Ira Mason, one of the union's leading lights since the turn of the century, was the party's candidate in civic elections in Ward Five. George Borland, another prominent leader of Local 83, was quoted in the *Citizen* on 15 September 1922 as saying that "Labour must supplement its industrial policy by political action."

The carpenters were the staunchest supporters of independent labour action in the city. In October, 1923, George Collins of Local 83 spoke strongly in favour of a motion calling on labour to contest a provincial by-election, and unite with delegates from the Trades and Labor Council, the United Workmen's Association, the Workers' Party, the Bricklayers' Union and the Labor Party to form the Central Council of Labor for Political Action (affiliated with the Canadian Labor Party). Carpenters were prominent among those who founded a local branch of the Canadian Labor Party in 1924. Comments from prominent carpenters in the *Citizen* on 25 July 1924 and 3 April 1925 criticized the local Trades and Labor Council for its inaction over such major labour cases as the trial of the coal miners' leader, J.B. McLachlan. In 1926, when the Halifax Trades and Labor Council elected a communist as its head, the carpenters (taking a position opposed by almost all other Halifax unions, including the printers, longshoremen, street railwaymen, painters, plumbers, railwaymen and electrical workers) wrote over the signature of William G. Hiscock, the recording secretary, to the *Evening Mail* on 9 March 1926: "The Carpenters Union Local 83, wish to state that they have every intention of standing back of the Trades and Labor Council of Halifax. We also wish to contradict the statement made by the Citizen, that the Trades and Labor Council was run by Communists." Such a defence of the Labor Council could only have been mounted on the basis of substantial growth in left-wing sentiment within the union.

How can this radicalism be explained, and why did it leave no permanent mark on Halifax after more than a decade of intensive activity? There are two answers. One is the depth of the economic crisis which forced many carpenters, including most of the radicals in Local 83, to leave Halifax in the 1920s. A second is the contradictory nature of the craft tradition itself.

Despite the 1919 strike, Halifax's construction in that year boomed; a sum of $5,194,805 in building permits was issued, a record high. By 1923, the total had dropped to $378,699, and by 1925 it had only partially recovered to $1,035,564. These estimates of construction activity convey a sense of the second Halifax Disaster which building craftsmen faced after Reconstruction stopped. According to the *Census*, in 1921, 644 Halifax carpenters earned $1,006 per year, working, on average, 42.46 weeks. In 1931, 593 Halifax carpenters earned $889 per year, working, on average, 38.29 weeks. The wage gaps between the crafts had widened, with electricians and wiremen earning almost double the amount commanded by plasterers and painters, and 54% more than the carpenters. (In 1921 carpenters in Halifax reported higher average earnings than electricians and wiremen.)

All the building crafts suffered from the collapse of the Halifax construction industry, but the carpenters were probably the hardest hit. The crisis of the building trades divided the crafts between those who managed to maintain or even slightly improve their standards (the plumbers and electricians) and those whose standards collapsed (the carpenters, painters and plasterers). Crafts in which apprenticeship had declined, entry requirements for new capital were small, and rural craftsmen were active, suffered bitterly. Those in which apprenticeship persisted, entry requirements for new capital were substantial, and rural craftsmen had no expertise, maintained their position. Divisions flourished on this terrain. Surveying the ruins of the city's once united and effective labour movement in the *Citizen* on 3 April 1925, George Collins of Local 83 remarked, "The Trades and Labor Council in Halifax is like a house divided against itself; there is no unity among the different organizations. We love the word Brotherhood, but Brotherhood does not exist...."

The craft traditions of the nineteenth-century city had been overwhelmingly protective in nature. They were based upon the exclusion of non-craftsmen through the restriction of entry to the crafts. In the first quarter of the twentieth century this exclusivist tendency, although hardly absent, was subordinated to a more pronounced development of common feeling with all labour, whether skilled or unskilled. When the labour market was relatively tight, as in 1913 or 1919, unionized carpenters sought not the exclusion of the rural and other migrant workers, but their enlistment in the ranks. But as the carpenters' position worsened in the 1920s, the remaining craftsmen turned back to this old strategy and did their best to safeguard what few remaining privileges they enjoyed in the market.

After 1919, Halifax craftsmen returned again and again to the same theme: we must be protected, they said, from the migrant, the handyman, and the botch. After pointing out that in order to deal successfully with the economic difficulties of the 1920s, craftsmen must regard their union as something sacred, J.T. McGrath, Local 83's business agent, noted in the *Citizen* on 19 March 1920: "Another difficulty which we have to contend with in our organization is the unskilled mechanic, which some of our local contractors thrust upon us and themselves also, and then raise the cry that we take them in our union and expect them to get the same pass as a good man.... Now, if the employers would reach an agreement with the men whereby they would refrain from hiring these wood butchers, the unions would soon eliminate them from their ranks, and I for one would guarantee that the price of fish and hay would decline perceptibly. It would also tend to entice a better standard of skill to gather on our shores. Let the farmers and fishermen abide where glory dwelleth.... Both employers and mechanics should get together and eliminate the botch. He will be needed in his own line of work. There will be lots of it for the handy man and unskilled worker." Was it fair, it was asked in the same paper on 21 May 1920, that first-class carpenters should be receiving less than other mechanics? What could be done with men "who are not carpenters," who were supplied with tools, and who worked on such public projects as schools at the paltry rate of 45-55¢ per hour, while "the mechanic has to correct their mistakes"?

Contractors, who themselves suffered from the collapse of the construction industry, were not slow to perceive the carpenters' weakness. "When industrial stagnation struck the city and a large surplus labour supply was on the market, the employers undertook to institute an arbitrary cut in wages," the *Citizen* remembered later in 1923. In 1921, the *Citizen* reported on 1 July, all carpenters employed on an alteration job in the city were laid off by the boss; he promptly hired new carpenters, "outside men who just came in to do his job, while taxpayers of this city are walking the streets." Refusing the "dictation" of the Halifax men, the contractor adopted the nine-hour day. "Like the rest of the building trades, the Carpenters have been working on the eight hour basis. But after the industrial depression set in and a number of building tradesmen were discharged, some employers took advantage of the situation and cut wages as well as lengthened hours, with the result that in some cases a nine hour day has been foisted upon the unorganized workers," reported the *Citizen* in 1921. Local 83 petitioned City Council to require contractors now working a nine-hour day to revert to the eight-hour system. City Council mislaid the resolution, discussed it after a lapse of three months, and did nothing.

In October, 1921, the contractors informed the building trades unions that the 1919 contract was to be re-opened in December, but they did not propose to negotiate the coming wage reductions.

By January 1922 the contract was reported no longer to be in working order. The Building Trades Council had collapsed, and separate agreements were imposed on each trade. The painters were cut from 66¢ to 55¢ per hour, and individual contractors began paying carpenters at this same low rate. While negotiations proceeded, A.A. McDonald, the president of the Builders' Exchange, slashed the wages of carpenters doing rough work on one of his jobs from 66¢ to 40¢ per hour. The wage scale finally arrived at was 57¢ per hour, but individual contractors broke the scale with impunity. Contractors at work at Dalhousie University were reported in June 1923 to be refusing jobs to city men and gave work to outsiders who would work for less. One employer was reported taking advantage of the "laws of supply and demand" by paying carpenters 25¢ per hour in July 1922.

The carpenters found themselves in roughly the same position as the coal miners in their great struggles of the 1920s—defending a postwar wage settlement with less and less success as unemployment undermined living standards and working-class unity. Like the coal miners, some saw in their plight a general indictment of the system as a whole. After noting A.A. McDonald's wage cuts, one commentator remarked in the *Citizen* on 22 July 1922, "this illustration is simply another reminder to the workers what they can expect when such men are placed in the position of dictator. The bourgeoisie object to a dictatorship of the proletariat; the sooner the workers object to the dictatorship of the bloodsucker, the better it will be for humanity." One carpenter suggested in the same newspaper on 2 March 1923 that "until they were beaten down into a starvation wage," trade unions had not been so anxious about the kind of government they wanted. "They formed committees and negotiated with the contractors or the business men and the boss, so to speak, and they were refused a fair wage, and were beaten to their knees by the so-called capitalistic bosses. Now the workers have decided to play the political game, to decide what kind of government they should have." Why the growth of communism in Halifax? "There must be a cause, and the cause is to be found in the industrial depression, the starvation and destitution of the working class. We are called ugly names because we refused to starve in a peaceable manner.... The system of capitalism has sown the seeds of distress and starvation, misery and despair. Now it must reap the whirlwind."

It is by no means clear how many carpenters would have identified with this position, although Local 83's consistent support of the left until 1927 suggests that these sentiments were held by a number of the union's members. And what became of this forgotten Halifax radicalism of the 1920s? It moved to the United States.

A mass emigration of carpenters in the 1920s undermined the growth of radical opinion. The chief attraction was the far higher level of pay and the steadiness of work. "How can carpenters in the United States be paid $1.10 an hour while in Halifax the union rate is only 57¢ an hour?" asked the *Citizen* on 10 April 1925. Numerous Halifax carpenters decided to investigate the mystery personally. John McGrath, Local 83's business agent, moved in 1920 to Lawrence, Massachusetts. J.W. Robson, financial secretary, packed his kit for Ottawa in 1922. George Borland, one of the Labor Party's staunchest supporters, moved the same year to New York; Ken Poole, likewise a Labor supporter and a delegate from Local 83 to the Labor Council, to Massachusetts. Walter Bottomley, secretary of the Labor Council and Local 83, moved in 1923 to Long Island, New York. Ernest Appleby, vice-president of Local 83, city resident for 23 years, and a strong advocate of labour politics, moved in 1923 to Medford, Massachusetts.

"One by one the skilled craftsmen are leaving the city, and it will be only a question of time when wages will have to be increased to keep the best mechanics from migrating to industrial centres, where work is plentiful and wages are adequate," the *Citizen* noted on 15 September 1922. As it observed on 20 April 1923, "Not only are these men skilled mechanics, but they have taken a deep interest in both the industrial and political movements of Labor, and their going has left the movement that much weaker."

Out-migration possibly affected radicals more than others; it certainly meant that those radicals who remained were playing before a dwindling and demoralized audience. Their constituency had moved away, and the labour politics of the early 1920s did not survive. As the historian John Manley notes of the Halifax communists, their success in the Labor Council meant less than it appeared, because by that time the Council itself was greatly reduced in numbers and influence, and the withdrawal of many unions left it a penniless rump by mid-1926.[12]

In this atmosphere of profound demoralization, the achievements of 1919 were undermined one by one. Unlike the coal miners, individual carpenters could win large economic gains for themselves within their trade by moving away, and they did so in large numbers. The militancy of 1919 and the political radicalism of 1919-1926 both dissipated in the all-encompassing gloom which covered the region in the late 1920s. Among these workers they have never reappeared.

The decline of class politics and labour militancy was experienced across Canada, but Halifax probably represented an extreme case, in which the labour movement was so gravely damaged by the crisis that it lost even the memory of important and significant achievements. Two generations of carpenters, each with its own leaders and ideas, had shaped the response of the craft to the drastic changes of the early twentieth century. They had taken the craftsmen far beyond their nineteenth-century traditions, had built a significant movement of protest, and had developed a working-class movement in the city. But no one built on their achievements or took up their cause. Elsewhere an enfeebled labour movement provided a sense of continuity between one generation of labour activists and the next. In Halifax, it was far less possible to do this. Most of the links had been broken.

As Local 83 began to move towards its modern strategy of managing the labour market through control of hiring in the late 1920s, it moved away from the union's tradition of political activism and militancy, and towards a strategy of "business unionism." This strategy was not an integral part of "craft unionism," for Local 83's history demonstrates, if nothing else, how militant and politicized the approaches of craft unionism can be.

Walter Galenson, the historian of the United Brotherhood of Carpenters and Joiners of America, summarizes the conventional view of the craft union when he writes, "The Carpenters were not organized to benefit society ... nor to help labour as a whole, or even to assist the other building trades unions. They were organized for the sole purpose of benefitting themselves. The history of the Carpenters is a stormy one, the story of a powerful organization protecting its own interests at almost any cost...."[13] The carpenters, he says, always turned a deaf ear to the wild-eyed theorists or the followers of misty Utopias.[14]

Selig Perlman, in his classic work on the outlook of the American Federation of Labor, described its philosophy as being based on a consciousness of limited job opportunities—so that any individual could occupy a job only if he obeyed the common rules laid down by his union. (He called this approach "job conscious trade unionism.") The safest way to assure this group control was to make the union the virtual owner and administrator of the jobs. This narrow emphasis on control of the job, he suggested, was far more important than an awareness of labour's position in society.[15]

We cannot recognize many features of Local 83's history from 1885-1925 in Galenson's or Perlman's portraits. The hallmarks of job-conscious "business unionism"—the strategies of "capturing" jobs and maintaining a relatively passive rank-and-file membership, endless jurisdictional struggles with other unions, avoidance of struggles involving a broader labour unity, centralization of all important trade union functions in the business agent rather than rank-and-file shop stewards, rejection of oppositional politics—are all either completely missing or present only in the most rudimentary forms.

Yet after 1925 these portraits describe the local reality more exactly. Part of the reason lay in the centralization of power within the international union, a process which had moved ahead markedly by 1917 (ironically to suit the more militant style of the age). But the more important reasons lay within the history of the Halifax carpenters themselves. In the first quarter of the twentieth century the carpenters had, to a surprising extent, identified themselves with the Halifax labour movement; now a new generation identified their movement far more narrowly, emphasizing the particular interests of carpenters and building tradesmen and not those of labour as a class. Such pragmatism was a response to the savage defeat suffered by the labour movement in the 1920s, and eventually seemed to be the only possible form craft unionism could take. This transition to a new approach preserved, under a completely new leadership, the institution; it did not preserve its reforming spirit, which fell as one more casualty to the crisis of the region in the 1920s.

4

The Emergence of Industrial Legality
1926-1952

He also reported Unions are accused of being run by union bosses. This he said is partly true but it's because the members lack participation at the union meetings...and also they lack knowledge of their constitution and union procedures.

— Bro. Kelsie reports on a seminar on unions,
Minutes, 21 November 1972

The great theme of the history of Local 83 from 1926 to the present is the triumph of industrial legality, a formal, legally enforced system of relations between labour, capital and the state. The emergence and growth of this system in the period after the 1920s redefined the world of the carpenters as thoroughly as had the earlier transition to consolidated capitalism.

Many authorities argue that this new system was born in 1944, with the establishment of legal recognition of the rights of private sector workers to organize, bargain collectively, and go on strike, through a federal order-in-council called PC 1003.[1] Yet it seems more accurate to see PC 1003 not as the *birth* of a new system, but the *extension* of an old one. Many important aspects of industrial legality—the check-off, growing bureaucracy, grievance procedures, regular contract negotiations—were in place in District 26 of the United Mine Workers of America, for instance, well before the Great Depression. In construction, the best birth date appears to be 1936, when passage of Industrial Standards Acts made wage rates achieved through collective bargaining legally binding.

Industrial legality meant that capital had to share power with labour and the state. It had to recognize unions, bargain in ways that were laid down in statutes, and pay the wages set out by law. Construction companies no longer had the right to run building sites just as they chose, and they had to operate within an industry directly influenced by housing, labour, and fiscal policies adopted by governments at all three levels. The most successful contractors fed directly from the hand of the state, for it was in this period that rapidly expanding institutions of government required buildings as never before.

The new system meant big changes for labour as well. Industrial legality emphasized the carrot, not the stick. It worked by persuading workers and their unions to consent to the new rules of the industrial game.

There were real and immediate benefits. Unionized workers won protection in the labour market and much higher wages. Their unions had the legal power to make companies listen. A contractor could not just decide to reduce wages, as in Halifax in the early 1920s and 1930s. He could not just fire employees. Eventually he even had to help organize the union, by co-operating with the check-off of union dues from his employees—even his non-union employees.

The drawbacks became clear afterwards. Industrial legality changed how unions worked, in ways which tended to take power from the ordinary worker and put it in the hands of elected and, increasingly, appointed officers. It forced the development of "professionalism" in labour circles. Decisions once made by shop stewards were now made by labour lawyers. The business agent and the international representative, men who lived their lives in this environment of labour laws and bargaining techniques, came naturally to dominate the union. In old-fashioned industrial relations, workers, about to go on strike, asked, "Are we stronger than our employers? How long can we hold out?" Now they had to ask, "Does this conflict with the collective agreement? When does this go before the conciliation board? How can we sell this politically?"

The price tag of the new system was that unions had to change the way they worked. They had to narrow their objectives. Bread-and-butter issues, particularly wages, dominated union functions, while old political ideals faded.

Walter Galenson, the official historian of the Brotherhood, captures the new spirit of trade unionism when he cites a revealing comment from John Williams, one of the Brotherhood's early presidents. "The worker has come to look upon the United Brotherhood as a vast business institution. Sentiment, which was a potent factor in the determination of my attitude toward it, has given way to a colder calculation of its virtues—to a more practical measuring of its value, and I must say that the contemplation from this viewpoint has caused the Brotherhood to take a firmer hold than ever on my allegiance and affection."[2]

From the perspective of this new kind of business unionism, a trade union had two main objectives: better wages and providing jobs. Everything else was secondary. The union's basic function was the selling of labour to contractors. The union headquarters became a hiring hall, and controlling jobs became one of the union's biggest concerns. Unions now fought fiercely among themselves over who would enjoy jurisdiction in the many grey areas that the construction industry produced. With the check-off, there was a direct relationship between the success of locals in defending their turf and the local's economic health. Business agents had to protect the local's jobs to protect their own positions.

The new idea of legal certification, by which safeguards and restrictions were placed on the very existence of a union in the workplace, meant that union leaders turned away from mobilizing and organizing and towards the juridical arena of labour boards. As two authorities on modern industrial relations remark, "In this context, different skills were necessary; it was crucial above all to know the law—legal rights, procedures, precedents, etc. These activities tended to foster a legalistic practice and consciousness in which union rights appeared as privileges bestowed by the state rather than democratic freedoms won and to be defended by collective struggle."[3] Canada's industrial relations legislation went even further than the American legislation it was modelled after, by forbidding strikes and lockouts during negotiations and throughout the term of the agreement, and by proscribing unfair labour practices by unions.[4]

For the state, the new system meant the possibility of political regulation of labour and a far greater degree of control over economic life. Initially, this was almost completely beneficial. Apprenticeship had languished in the period 1830-1860 and never recovered; now the provincial government, through an Apprenticeship Act, brought it back. Wages had been under attack throughout the first three decades of the twentieth century. Now the provincial government would give the force of law to the bargains made between contractors and employees. Housing had been privately controlled and was often priced too high for masses of people. Now the federal government would help subsidize inexpensive housing through the Central Mortgage and Housing Corporation. Trade unions had been attacked. Now they would be certified and employers would have to accept them. Trade unionists once had to struggle just to be listened to. Now they were part of the very machinery of government, sitting on boards, commissions, conciliation hearings...

The costs only became apparent after the system had become entrenched. The revival of apprenticeship did not mean the revival of the craft, because apprentices were trained in the public educational system and did not feel any debt to the union. Wage standards could be established by government, but so could wage controls. The benevolent hand which turned on the tap of government spending on housing could, at other times, just as easily turn it off. Certification gave authorities other than the workers the right to determine the appropriate bargaining unit— and this decision could be manipulated to suit the needs of the moment. Trade unionists might be admitted through the state's front door, but only a few—and their very admission seemed to distance them from the people they led.

The system imposed long-term costs that nobody fully foresaw in the 1930s and 1940s. It guaranteed "free collective bargaining" but imposed new and much harsher restrictions on what the average member of a union could do. Presented as an even-handed compromise between capital and labour, the system nevertheless left capital with its basic power—the right to say when, where and how work was to take place—intact.

Local 83's history since the 1920s has been moulded by the system of industrial legality. It took shape in the 1920s and 1930s, was consolidated in the 1940s, and has reigned supreme ever since.

One basic theme underlying the entire period is the waning of democracy within the union. The shop stewards, once the major union organizers in the various workplaces, gradually became ineffective. Power gravitated to the full-time officials and international representatives. The membership lost power and became bored. Business agents prospered and alternative politics withered.

Local 83's records provide us with an unusually detailed and vivid sense of this transition to business unionism, but it is important to remember the context of such developments if we are not to judge the union unfairly. Much of the history of the Local was no longer under local control. It is difficult to say what, if anything, the carpenters might have done to stop the process. Withdrawal from the system of industrial legality established in the 1930s and 1940s would have been a short route to oblivion. Participation meant accepting its basic ground rules.

It is often argued that the Great Depression made little difference to Maritimers because it came on the heels of the regional economic collapse of the 1920s. But, for construction workers at least, this is not quite the case. There was just enough time for workers to rebuild their unions and re-establish some standard rates before the next crisis swept these accomplishments away.

From 1926 to 1929 the local building economy had revived considerably. In the very year of the Great Crash, the local business agent, obviously no prophet, described conditions as "very favourable" and suggested this would continue.

After the depths of the slump in the 1920s, carpenters found themselves working on the new Lord Nelson Hotel and new immigration facilities. There was work, too, at Dalhousie University, a new cold storage plant, the Victoria General Hospital, and the Technical School. In these conditions of partial economic recovery, construction unions were able to make rapid gains.

In the period 1926-1931, the years before the Great Depression hit the Halifax carpenters with full force, the union moved a long way towards industrial legality. This was suggested by four things: the tightening of controls over jobs (partly through a working card system established by the Building Trades Council), the reliance upon Fair Wages legislation, the vigorous rejection of past political activism, and the rise of the business agent to the leading position in the union.

Local 83 was able to increase its membership by 30% between 1926 and 1928, and by November, 1928, claimed over 200 members. (This was, of course, far short of the levels in 1919 and 1920.) On 20 December 1929, the *Citizen* noted that Local 83, with 420 members, was the second largest union in the city. The building craftsmen were determined to win back the ground lost after 1919. On the urging of Local 56 of the Plumbers and Steamfitters, the Building Trades Council was reorganized in 1927 to settle all questions arising from time to time in connection with wages and conditions of labour. This new Council was not formed as a loose federation of unions, but as a potent force for disciplining and co-ordinating the labour market. For the first time Halifax unions sought to exert strict control over building sites through a system of quarterly working cards. By 1 July, the *Citizen* noted, the members of all unions affiliated with the Building Trades Council had been given working cards, "and union men will not be permitted to work on jobs where non-union men are employed." As a result of the new card system, reported the *Citizen*, "there has been much activity among non-unionists to become members of the various unions, and it is expected that within the next few weeks the membership of the unions in the building trades will be considerably augmented."

The union fought hard to control access to jobs. Discussions within Local 83 focussed on the building of the Lord Nelson Hotel. Gaining control over the Lord Nelson site was crucial, they argued, because it would bring within the union all those outside carpenters who were gathering at the hotel project for work. The Minutes for 3 April 1928 record that Montreal carpenters on the site were told to get working cards (at 25¢ per month) or leave.

All the city's construction jobs were monitored closely. When non-unionists were employed, the business agent was ready to tell employers the job would be "pulled" unless non-unionists were either discharged or became members. The contractors building the new Capitol Theatre, for example, were warned on 8 April 1930 that they would have "till Monday to make it a Union Job and if not the Job would be pulled on Tuesday morning...." On 3 February 1931, Local 83 dealt with non-unionists in the employ of the McDougald Construction Company on the Court House site by resolving "that no member of Local 83 go to work with McD. Cons. Co. until told to do so by the Bus. Agent. Penalty $25.00 fine."

The union's strict insistence on both the closed shop and the card system was new, and it was effective. Contractors began to complain of the scarcity of skilled labour in Halifax. The union had a ready reply: the supply of labour would be plentiful for any contractor who paid the union rate.

Secondly, new emphasis was placed on the enforcement of Fair Wages legislation, through which the federal government had established minimum labour standards and conditions for contractors on government jobs. Local 83 pressed Peter Heenan, Minister of Labour, to impose fair wage guidelines on work at the new immigration facilities, and was equally strenuous in its efforts to apply such standards to the construction of the Civic Exhibition, the new CNR hotel, and construction of a new icebreaker.

Applying pressure to politicians to treat the carpenters fairly was now the extent of the Local's political activism, for the tide had turned massively against the political activists who had formerly led the union. Ralph Eisnor, the leading advocate of independent labour politics, was no longer president, and those who succeeded him did not share his political vision. The international Brotherhood as a whole was turning to a far more conservative style of trade unionism and had occupied itself in the 1920s with expelling members accused of radicalism. Its general representative in Halifax, Pat Green, had evidently been mandated to carry out the same policies on a local level. Green was of the opinion that industrial unionism had always been a failure, whereas craft unions under the banner of the international movement were generally successful. He was critical of the left-wing sentiment which had characterized the union. When Local 83 received a communication from the Manitoba Independent Labor Party on 2 April 1929, it passed an unusual motion that the communication "be thrown in the waste Paper Basket." Although some of the union's senior members (such as Ira Mason, S.J. Hatcher, and Harry Simpson) continued to raise general political points, the Local viewed them with impatience, resolving, for example, to throw into the same basket a resolution touching on government control of the Port of Halifax.

Perhaps the most important new development was the emergence of the business agent. Local 83 had had such agents before; but, from what can be gleaned from incomplete historical records on this question, the position was generally temporary, poorly paid, and relatively powerless. The position created on 6 November 1928, however, carried with it a reasonable salary and the power to bestow jobs upon members. The business agent became the main figure in the union, and shop stewards, correspondingly, were now found only in a few spots, as the Minutes on 5 March 1929 confirmed explicitly. In this respect, Halifax had gone further than other centres. A stranger in the Local expressed his astonishment on 18 March 1930 at the way in which members disregarded overtime rules in his workplace, and asked who the shop steward was; he was surprised to learn that there was none.

Underlying the success of the union as it flourished briefly at the end of the 1920s was the brief recovery of the building market. After the wage reductions of 1922—from 66¢ to 55¢—the carpenters had returned to win two wage increases in 1927 (of 2¢ and 3¢ respectively) to bring the scale to 60¢. Pat Green reminded the Local that even with this increase, the "Carpenters' scale in this city is the lowest in Canada, possibly with one exception." In 1928 after demanding 70¢, the Local signed an agreement with the Exchange for 66¢. This was seen as a watershed by the *Citizen* on 4 May 1928. "While the increase in wages is recognized as comparatively small," the paper noted, "the unions have been considerably increased in membership and improvement in working conditions has been gained. Besides this the unions' right to recognition has been firmly established, the employers being satisfied that collective bargaining is the right and proper way of adjusting differences between employers and employees in respect to wages and working conditions." In May, 1929, the September *Labour Gazette* reports, Local 83 and the Exchange signed an agreement raising wages to 73¢ per hour, which also specified that no carpenter was to work for less, except by permission of the union.

The Local was lucky to have won an agreement early in 1929, for with the advent of the Depression employers started to reverse the gains achieved in 1928 and 1929.

The Depression was slow to affect Halifax, judging at least from the city's business press, but when it finally arrived its impact was dramatic. As the *Commerical News* reported in January, 1935, construction in the city, which measured over $5.2 million in 1929, decreased to only one-tenth that amount in 1933. The picture was made even more gloomy by the absence of any long-term construction projects. Most of the jobs in 1933 consisted of repair work, providing short-term employment at best. The worst season was 1934, a year in which, one Halifax contractor remembers, one put "patches over patches."

Slowly, inevitably, conditions for Halifax carpenters worsened. In 1929, employers once again began importing large numbers of outside workers. Although the city had imposed a head tax on such workmen, it was easily evaded. The *Citizen* complained on 27 December 1929 that "outside workers are continually coming into the city and getting jobs while residents and taxpayers are compelled to walk the streets looking for work. It is not known how many of these outsiders pay the poll tax, but it is said that there are quite a number who do not." And the Minutes suggest that as early as 1929 outsiders were once again flocking to Halifax and breaking the union's rates. On 21 June 1931, the *Citizen* reported on Labor Council protests over discrimination against members of Local 83 by the city engineer, and on claims that "outsiders were given work while Halifax citizens walked the streets."

By 1932 the situation had grown even more grave. J.C. Beattie, secretary of Local 83, asked the Labor Council in March to send a committee to City Hall "to try and put a stop to outside contractors and labour coming into Halifax and doing practically all the residential contracting in the city." Small victories in the battle against the influx of labour—such as forcing the School Board to insert a fair wages clause in the contract for additions to Alexandra School—were few and far between. The union passed resolution after resolution, such as that on 20 November 1934 "against outside labor coming into Halifax until conditions are better," with little effect.

Everywhere the craft was threatened with disorganization. The Building Trades Council, which had been hailed as such a major reform in construction hiring, collapsed in 1930. The Capitol Theatre, employing non-unionists, could not be shut down, and finally Local 83 merely posted it as being "unfair to labor" in *The Carpenter*. The July 1931 issue of the Brotherhood's journal contained a "stay away" notice from the Local. With a decreasing membership and a large proportion of members in arrears, even the services of the business agent had to be dispensed with in 1931, although the hesitation with which this step was taken, and the attempts made by Local 83 in the very depths of the Depression to hire a business agent, even for just three months, suggested how central the position had become.

The crisis of the construction industry led to brutal wage cuts. Contractors trying to survive the Depression themselves had little choice. As early as 1929, the Exchange was dividing the crafts into the strong and the weak, placing the painters, carpenters, and labourers among those too weak to be given the increases granted others. When the Exchange refused to these three groups the increases it had granted to others, the carpenters were indignant. "The employers tried their best to force the carpenters to go on strike," remarked one carpenter in the *Citizen* on 18 July 1930, after the

Exchange had brought the rate for his trade down to 67½¢, "but the men, using their good judgement, refused . . . . If there is prosperity in the city of Halifax, then the Carpenters, Painters and Laborers are entitled to their share of it as well as the other building tradesmen, and have just as good a right to it as the Builders' Exchange. What more can we do? Would you suggest that we buy dynamite, high explosive, poison gas and machine guns and force our rights?"

But such incendiary talk and the Local's official threats of "drastic action" were stilled as the gravity of the situation became apparent. The painters, who did fight a strike against the Exchange, were beaten completely, and their union forced out of existence.

In 1932 the Exchange proposed extensive wage cuts of between 11% and 20% for the building trades (cutting the carpenters from 73¢ to 65¢). The response of the union was to suggest a reduction of 10% and a 40-hour week. The union was in a weak position, and the employers knew it. They imposed an old-fashioned, unilateral wage reduction. "In former years," complained one trade unionist in the *Citizen* on 6 May, "the wage rates were settled by negotiations, but this year the Exchange set their rates at a dinner at the Lord Nelson Hotel, and the men feel rightly or wrongly that the drastic cuts were inspired by the spirit of retaliation." Prior to 1932, another was to comment the following year, "the general policy followed, concerning working conditions was by a conference between the employers and their employees, but since that date there appears to be only one side to the wage question, and that is the employers' side. In effect it is 'your wages will be so much; take it or leave it.'"

The strongest trades—the bricklayers, plasterers, and electrical workers—went on strike against the reductions on 2 May. After the strike ended on 12 May, and after the intervention of M.S. Campbell of the federal Department of Labour, the reduction had been reduced to 10% for at least 12 months, on the understanding that when negotiations for all the building trades resumed in 1933 they would be based on the 1931 rates. However, the Exchange forced further reductions in 1933, which reduced the wages of carpenters to 55¢ per hour.

"We have all heard of 10 and even 20 per cent wage and salary cuts," the *Citizen* said on 19 May 1933, "but when a 30 per cent reduction is asked for it is a matter for very serious consideration." Local 83 was outraged by this reduction, and spent the next three years agitating for its repeal.

Carpenters felt themselves being reduced to the status of common labourers. Their position as honourable mechanics was crumbling. One contractor, J.P. Porter & Sons, made this explicit in June, 1932, by classifying all carpentry work as "timber work" to be paid at 50¢ per hour. Forced onto relief, carpenters were humiliated by the thought that they would be reduced to the unskilled labour that relief projects usually required. Local 83 appealed through the Labor Council for a program for skilled labour "whereby skilled mechanics will be afforded employment as well as the common labourer."

The real question here was one of craft pride. Carpenters were reluctant to admit that the mechanics' place in society had declined so far. The *Citizen* explained their position eloquently. "Skilled mechanics will not accept pick and shovel work," the labour weekly argued on 1 December 1933. "There are scores of useful and necessary public [works] that could be and should be undertaken, thus enabling the mechanical class to find something to do at their respective callings, rather than to be offered jobs that are, to say the least, beyond the skilled men of the Building Trades. Let us get away from mere pick and shovel work. The mechanic has just as much right to refuse this type of employment as has the office clerk or the business man. The skilled worker is not asking for charity, and pick and shovel work is absolute charity—call it by any other name if you will." "It is all very well," the *Citizen* said two weeks later, "to say that a man should take any kind of job rather than to remain idle. That is unsound philosophy, and besides, it is not facing the real unemployment situation."

The emergence of industrial legality can only be appreciated if it is put in this context of a craft disintegrating in the Depression. It emerged partly from the demands of contractors for protection from outside competitors and partly from new demands of labour for work and decent wages.

For labour, a new emphasis on the state did not mean the rebirth of independent labour politics. Local 83 wanted specific reforms, not radical political change. First, it wanted direct relief, of a type appropriate to mechanics, through federal and provincial construction projects. Second, it wanted civic and provincial governments to protect local labour through the preferential hiring of local workers. Finally, it wanted all three levels of government to protect their wage rates, through Fair Wage and Industrial Standards legislation. Taken singly, none of these reforms was all that impressive; together, they amounted to a change in the position of the state in the world of industrial relations.

The government, Local 83 believed, had to come up with major building projects. The only big project underway in 1934 was the construction of Pier B at a cost of $1 million. The waterfront site, reported the March 1934 *Commercial News*, was "the only large construction work being carried on," and otherwise "building construction has been practically at a standstill."

By the end of 1935, the situation had improved somewhat. Some house builders were back at work, and construction was underway at the navy dockyards and the south end terminals. The best news, however, came from the federal and provincial governments. Nearly $1 million worth of manpower and materials was earmarked for waterfront projects, and a further million for a new federal building on Hollis Street. In addition, a new provincial building was slated for Bedford Row. "It looks like a busy summer for the building tradesmen," noted the *Citizen* on 5 July 1935. "The erection of these two big buildings will mean a stimulus to the building industry in Halifax. That's what we want—more building construction. If the building trades are prospering, it means that business in general will pick up." In June, 1935, the *Commercial News* reported the Board of Trade's optimistic view that the city had turned the corner, and that "conditions were much improved over last year."

Preferential hiring of local workers was demanded more fiercely in the Depression than ever before, and finally there were results. The outside craftsmen would from now on be required by the City Charter to pay a tax of $10 before commencing work in Halifax. (Local 83 charged a "tax" as well: on 5 April 1938 we read of Montreal carpenters working on Bloomingdale Terrace having to pay a "working tax" of 75¢ per month.) Under the Nova Scotia Labour Act in 1933, any person or corporation employing 25 or more workers was forbidden to hire anyone who had not been a resident of Nova Scotia for at least one year, unless that person produced a certificate from the Government Employment Agent or the Municipal Clerk in the place where he was to be employed, stating there were no unemployed persons there capable and willing to do the work. Nova Scotia carpenters were to be given preference in hiring.

Neither of these two laws, however, was as radical in its scope as the Industrial Standards Act, which came into effect in 1936. This Act was brought about to meet the needs of both contractors and building craftsmen. Even the business press recognized the terrible vulnerability of Halifax construction workers in the 1930s. After outlining the minimum wage laws in other provinces, through which workers had been protected against the worst forms of wage-cutting, E.A. Saunders, secretary of the Board of Trade, remarked in the *Commercial News* of December, 1935, that wages paid by building contractors "particularly in the carpentry and painting trades are far from being satisfactory and a law similar to [that] I have outlined would be very desirable." Some wages legislation was desirable from the point of view of Halifax contractors, as a protection against "small contractors from outside districts coming into this city and bringing labour with them, paying a lower rate and, as a rule, for inferior work than [that done under] the wage scale agreed upon between the contractors and local unions." The *Commercial News* in October, 1936 interpreted the passage of the legislation primarily as a victory for "those who are engaged in different trades having established businesses and paying large taxes in the city."

Force of circumstance brought contractors and carpenters together in a common political project. Local 83 had long relied on federal Fair Wages Legislation, but this applied only to contractors on government work, and was not consistently enforced. The Industrial Standards Act, in contrast, was a breakthrough for labour, because it removed the competitive advantages enjoyed by outside contractors. George A. Smith, Local 83's president by this period, who was called "the father of the Industrial Standards legislation" by the *Citizen*, rightly called the Act "a forward step in labor legislation" and claimed it "marked a new era in the building trades in Halifax and Dartmouth." To a degree unknown since the nineteenth century, employers and employed seemed to be in agreement on a joint project which would protect their mutual interests. Their unity was symbolized by the joint petition they presented to Premier Angus L. Macdonald in the Spring of 1936, calling for the legislation.

The 1936 legislation, similar to a law under the same name enacted in Ontario in 1935, was the greatest structural change in the industry since the turn of the century. It applied only to the construction trades in Halifax and Dartmouth, where it had the effect of applying a standard, negotiated wage structure to the entire industry. On petition of employers or employees, the provincial Minister of Labour was empowered to convene a conference of people engaged in the industry to negotiate standard rates of wages and hours. The schedule that they came up with was to be published in the *Royal Gazette*, thereby becoming binding on all employers and employees in the industry, whether unionized or not, with the exception of employees of the provincial or municipal governments or related boards and commissions. Employers failing to honour the hours and wages established were liable to fines of $25 to $100 or three months in jail. An amendment the following year stipulated the law's application to any job valued at over $25 in labour and the cost of materials. On 2 September 1936 the *Royal Gazette* published the first four Orders-in-Council, governing electrical workers, plumbers and steamfitters, bricklayers, and carpenters. The carpenters' wages were set at 60¢, with provisions for an eight-hour day and overtime. In 1939, the Act was amended to set up a system of inspection.

It would be difficult to overstate the importance of this legislation. In one fell swoop it changed the whole complexion of the local building market. It resurrected the local contractors, who could once more play a leading role in construction projects. The traditional menace of the rural craftsmen threatened no longer.

And, crucially, the Act was enforced. "In the enforcement of the Act a limited amount of persuasion was used where the circumstances justified it," the Department of Labour claimed in 1939, "but whether persuasion or sterner methods were used, it has been made plain that the law must be respected. The manner of enforcing the law has not been questioned, the official representatives of the workers are not inclined to effect the desired results." At least five contractors were fined for violation of the Industrial Standards Act in 1938.

The 1936 Act represented, in this industry, the birth of industrial legality. It gave legal status to collective bargaining. Collective agreements had at one time been hit-and-miss affairs. After the 1919 agreement collapsed in the early 1920s, the contractors simply notified the workers that they were going to get lower wages. Now negotiated schedules would have the force of law.

The Act became the banner of Local 83, to be defended at all costs, even the cost of a Halifax law firm, now required to draft the complex agreements and try the complicated cases engendered by the Act. One case which reveals the importance of the Industrial Standards Act and the tenacity with which Local 83 defended it was the Local's attempt to force the Halifax Harbour Commission to observe the rates established by the Act. The carpenters employed by the Halifax Commission argued that they should come under the provisions of the Industrial Standards Act of 1936, but that since 1 June 1938 the Commissioners had been paying at a lower rate. Carpenters with the National Harbours Board (NHB) were receiving only 62¢ when they should, under provincial law, have been receiving 65¢. "Would you kindly investigate this matter," J.C. Beattie, Local 83's recording secretary, asked W.M. Dickson, the federal Deputy Minister of Labour, "and have it adjusted as soon as possible, thereby eliminating a whole lot of trouble that can so easily be avoided."[5] While the NHB evidently complied initially, by 1 June 1938 it was paying a lower wage than called for under the Act, and Beattie's "whole lot of trouble" took five years and countless letters and memoranda to unravel.

Local 83's skill in presenting its case to politicians in this affair was impressive. George Smith, president of both the Labor Council and the Local, got in touch with Gordon B. Isnor, the M.P.; Isnor took the case to R.O. Campney, the Chairman of the National Harbours Board.[6] Local 83 also applied directly to Norman McLeod Rogers in Ottawa to use his influence with the Board. Rogers passed the responsibility over to the National Harbours Board.

The NHB argued that the case hinged on whether the Industrial Standards Act applied to rates for steady, full-time employment, or rather (as it argued), if it governed only those rates payable for casual labour. When J.C. Beattie learned of the NHB's position, he wrote to Rogers, "The employees of the National Harbours Board cannot be considered as permanent employees for the simple reason they are liable to be laid off at any time being paid by the hour. In fact all the carpenters on the Board have been laid off, except the charge hands, from one to two weeks and in some cases longer since they secured their employment. We also know that while the Harbours Board does not wish to pay prevailing rates in Halifax they are doing so on the West Coast where the rates are much higher than here. All the large contractors in Halifax employ a number of carpenters the year round and must pay these men the prevailing rate of wages and this is all we are asking the National Harbours Board to do."[7]

The NHB, however, did not want to discuss any of these points with the government or the union. "[I]t is suggested that no good purpose will be served in continuing this correspondence," went one of the NHB's memoranda on this subject. "The matter has been fully and clearly covered in communications with the parties concerned...."[8] Commenting on this stubbornness, Gordon B. Isnor remarked to the Department of Labour, "the Board's attitude is one which is not conducive to bringing about the results your Department is seeking to maintain."[9]

The matter was far from settled in the eyes of Local 83, for if a crown corporation could break established rates, so could anybody. The Labor Council returned to this theme over and again. Less official attempts were made to discredit port manager R.W. Hendry who, one outraged Liberal worker wrote, "has run amuck among our best Liberal Workers, laying off some and over-working others and with-holding payment of over-time, threatening some and abusing others. . . . "[10] "It is indeed [regrettable] that I have again to protest on behalf of Local 83 that the wages paid by the Harbours Board in Halifax are below the prevailing wage," wrote J.C. Beattie in 1939. "Just why does this condition exist and for how much longer a time will it be allowed to exist? Organized Labour in Halifax wishes to know the final decision in this matter."[11] In 1941 the building tradesmen's mounting frustration was conveyed in a telegram sent by Beattie to the Minster of Labour:

> UNREST MOUNTING IN HMC DOCKYARD AND NATIONAL HARBOURS BOARD AND UNLESS THE INDUSTRIAL STANDARDS ACT RATE OF PAY THAT IS EIGHTY CENTS PER HOUR IS PAID ON BOTH JOBS ON OR BEFORE SEPTEMBER FIRST LOCAL UNION 83 UNITED BROTHERHOOD OF CARPENTERS WILL BE COMPELLED TO PLACE THE FEDERAL GOVERNMENT ON THE UNFAIR LIST AND TAKE APPROPRIATE ACTION TO BRING ABOUT AN ADJUSTMENT.[12]

"I might state," said Gordon Isnor to NHB officials in 1942, "that there appears to be a general atmosphere of dissatisfaction among the carpenters concerning the matter of their pay and I would ask you to review same."[13] Finally the carpenters working on the Halifax waterfront did receive the increase—five years after the case had first come to the attention of Ottawa.

This episode was relatively minor by itself—in most years the discrepancy in rates affected less than a dozen men—yet it says a lot about that new world of labour relations we have called "industrial legality." It was a world which required the establishment of standard rates, a capacity to write innumerable letters, and good political connections. It was a bureaucratic world, in which a wage case affecting some carpenters on the waterfront could lead to the creation of several fat files of official, not to say officious, correspondence.

By the end of the 1930s Local 83 had recovered from the acute crisis of 1933 and 1934. Under the capable and devoted leadership of George Smith (1894-1979), the Local in these years became the most important of the city's craft unions. Smith joined the Carpenters in 1929 and was chosen as a delegate to the Labor Council in 1930. He was elected president of Local 83 in 1931 and held that office for the following 17 years. He was elected president of the Labor Council in 1937 and held the office until he resigned in 1951. He was on the Nova Scotia provincial executive of the Trades and Labor Congress and served as its chairman for three years. He reorganized many of the city's unions, including the painters. By 1936, 18 unions were affiliated with the Labor Council, many of them organized by Smith. Like Arthur Lessell and Ralph Eisnor before him, Smith became the *de facto* spokesman for Halifax labour. As his obituary in 1979 noted, he held many important positions: representative of the Trades and Labor Congress, member of the minimum wage board from 1934 to 1948, director of the Central Mortgage and Housing Corporation, and member of the local advisory committee of the Unemployment Insurance Commission since its inception. He was a devoutly Christian man, socially conservative, a proponent of "sound and cautious agitation." It was wholly typical of him that when the Labor Forum, held weekly at the Labor Temple, took up the topic of the "League of Nations" in 1936, Smith remarked that "it would be better for the workers to discuss matters nearer home. What we need to discuss today . . . [are] our social problems, [how to] improve employment conditions; provide better homes for those unable to pay high rental."

Smith was a traditional craft unionist of the 1930s, but this did not necessarily mean he was right-wing. He presided over meetings of the local branch of the left-wing Canadian Seamen's Union, and when asked about the involvement of communists in it replied, "What we want is a good strong union. We are not concerned with 'isms'. . . . What we want is justice for the workers." Following his lead, Local 83 pitched in heavily with support for the Lockeport Lockout of 1939, regardless of the leadership provided by communists in that struggle. Smith adamantly rejected any thought of a tie with the Co-operative Commonwealth Federation (CCF) or any other labour party. In contrast with the next generation of labour leaders, however, he was perfectly willing to work with anyone to strengthen the position of craft unions and organize the unorganized. And Smith viewed with dismay some of the developments within the International Brotherhood which made it more difficult for anyone to challenge the increasingly entrenched leadership of President Hutcheson.

The late 1930s, thanks largely to the rescue efforts of the state, left Local 83 in a much stronger position than it had been in previously. Craft unionism in Halifax expanded—partly because of the competition from industrial unions organized under the Congress of Industrial Organizations, the CIO. Signs of recovery were everywhere from 1937 on: the hiring of a business agent on 3 August 1937, the re-establishment of the Building Trades Council on 21 March 1939. As *The Citizen* observed on 16 April 1937, Local 83 had "resumed its former status as one of the leading factors in the movement in this city, as well as one of its oldest members."

The Second World War brought an immense construction boom to Halifax and Dartmouth. New fortifications were required by the war, and new housing and defence installations in the ensuing peace. "Work was rushed on the great runways, the barracks, mess halls, hangars, and workshops at Eastern Passage, and in the meantime the city was thronged with young men in Air Force blue seeking billets and lodgings until there was accommodation at the field," writes Thomas Raddall in his history of Halifax.[14]

The War had a dramatic impact on Canadian society. Full employment after years of frustration and unemployment brought a wave of radical activism and militancy at the height of the war effort. Union membership shot up from 17.3 to 30.3% of the non-agricultural workforce. The Liberal government read opinion polls which put the socialist CCF ahead of both themselves and the Conservatives, and was quickly converted to a philosophy of broad social reform.

Labour became scarce. After the secretary of Local 83 received a query from the National Labour Supply Council as to whether men were available for employment, he was instructed on 1 May 1940 to reply, "all employed, majority working on war work, const., etc." There was a rapid rise in the level of activity: building permits, for example, climbed from just over $800,000 in 1943 to nearly $2,800,000 the following year.

The War also meant more state planning of the economy. Bodies like the Wartime Prices and Trade Board and the Regional War Labour Board now exerted direct power over the lives of the carpenters. An Order-in-Council of 1940 made it illegal for competing employers to entice workmen away from war production. Amendments the following year gave the government the power to make regulations to prevent the employment of persons in certain designated skilled or scarce trades except through employment offices.

In return for complying with the National Labour Code, which called for compulsory negotiation and conciliation instead of strikes, building tradesmen were rewarded with cost-of-living bonuses. (Those paid over $25 per week, for example, were to receive an additional $2.25.) Although local employers in the Exchange complained in the *Commercial News* of January 1945 that the cost-of-living bonuses had become part of the "basic wage," there was little they could do to change the situation. The appetite of the war economy was insatiable. It drew off materials and labour required for wartime housing construction, which in turn created a critical housing shortage.

The war economy's serious shortages of supplies and labour sparked protests from the Local. On 20 November 1945, Local 83 protested to Ottawa "as to shortage of Building Materials" and requested " a larger quota for the district." As for central planning of the labour market, the Local objected, in letters to the Prime Minister and the Minister of Labour in 1945, to the "transferring of Maritime workers when they should continue [in the factories] of Nova Scotia."

How to avoid a sudden decrease in production was the problem which haunted both contractors and workers. There was a striking contrast here between the First World War and the Second. The First was conducted with only the rudiments of a social policy; the Second with a whole-hearted commitment to co-ordinating the economy from the centre and bringing the trade union leadership into this process. Even employers thought that the state should direct the war economy and superintend the process of reconstruction. The Canadian Construction Association, as early as 1940, called upon the government to take definite precautions against the unsettled period it foresaw at the end of the War.

The War made a particular difference to Halifax carpenters in three specific ways. Wartime production brought controversial demands for longer hours of work. On 1 April 1941, Local 83 went on record as being opposed to any change in working hours, and insisted through the War on maintaining or improving on the pre-war standard. (In 1945, it demanded and received for the first time, the 40-hour week with the same weekly pay as the 44-hour week.)

Secondly, the war economy had little respect for traditional definitions of the craft. Carpenters found themselves working in greater numbers in marine settings, in the Dockyard, Shipyards, and the Dartmouth Slip. This entailed a number of thorny problems. One was that of maintaining the status of skilled men. In such settings as the Shipyards and Dockyard, "improvers" were put on carpentry work and paid at a lower rate than journeymen. The War also brought difficult working conditions in an authoritarian environment, as carpenters found themselves jolted across rough roads in military vehicles of dubious safety, and crating explosives at the Bedford Magazine.

Finally, state control over the labour market gave the union a measure of control within closed shops it had never enjoyed before. On 19 May 1942 the business agent was reported to be "endeavouring to organize a closed shop in shipwright shop Dockyard." When non-union carpenters were reported at H.M.C. Dockyard, the Local dashed off a protest letter to the Minister of Labour on 21 October 1942, noting the efforts "of Local officers to avert any trouble." Most importantly, private contractors, such as J.N. Kenny, Butler Brothers, and Anglin Norcross, were reported to be 100% organized in December, 1943. When a man working on Pier 21 refused to join the union, the Local got the assurance of "Co-operation from Bricklayers & Carpenters on job . . . that if he did not join by Wednesday noon, action will be taken." The war economy favoured the closed shop.

Labour's institutions responded to the challenge of the war economy. The most dramatic change was the organization of a separate local for marine carpenters by the Brotherhood in 1943-44. On 2 February 1943, Andrew Cooper, the Brotherhood's general organizer, reported that he had received permission from the General Executive Board "to organize a New Union in Halifax Shipyards & Dartmouth Slip." Local 83 agreed with this, but anxiously specified that the "Charter must state Halifax Shipyards & Dartmouth Slip *ONLY*." However, the Charter of Local 1405, granted in 1944, covered the Halifax Shipyards, H.M.C. Dockyard (with the exception of the carpenter shop), the Marine Slip, Purdy Brothers, T. Hagan and Company, and (most controversially) all woodworking mills in the vicinity of the city except the Brookfield Construction Co. mill on Mitchell Street.

The emergence of Local 1405 was a response to the new importance of the marine carpenters, but it raised as many problems as it solved. Jurisdictional disputes quickly broke out between the two locals, for military authorities shifted carpenters from marine to land construction with sublime indifference to the lines drawn by trade unions. Two locals, pressing close together in a small city and with a vague line of demarcation drawn between them, generated jurisdictional quarrels with effortless spontaneity.

Serious conflicts emerged in 1947, with Local 83 protesting against Local 1405's habit of charging a lower initiation fee as an inducement to members. Local 83 also wanted jurisdiction over local mills, and pointed to 1405's lack of success in this sphere. Only in 1950 was this simmering dispute ended, when the General Executive Board ruled that Local 1405 was to enjoy the jurisdiction established in 1944. On 7 February 1950, Local 83 decided to appeal this decision, but without result.

Another major development brought about by the War (which could be traced back to the effects of the Industrial Standards Act) was the extension of organization to rural areas of the Maritimes.

On 18 June, 1940, Local 83 decided to urge the International to come to organize lumber workers in Milton, Queens County, and on 17 August 1943 an urgent resolution passed instructing local headquarters that "unless something is done *at once* a great loss in Membership will be forthcoming if small towns are not organized by A.F. of L. Send organizer to Metag[h]an at once and view situation. (Appoint organizer at once.)" Local 83 thought its business agent, J.H. Dwyer, was the man for the job, and he eventually got it. Locals of the Brotherhood spread throughout rural Nova Scotia. This reflected partly the demands of local workers, at a time when enthusiasm for trade unions was running high in Canada, and partly the Brotherhood's anxiety to ward off a challenge from rival unions affiliated with the CIO.

Politically, the changes within Local 83 were less momentous. The union did not join the general stampede to the CCF, but it sympathized with the left more than is commonly remembered. It passed resolutions in favour of the Co-operative Movement and participated in its activities. Some sympathy towards the CCF was suggested by letters written to Clarie Gillis, CCF member from Cape Breton, exposing the $38,000 spent on remodelling a house for the military. (The most successful candidate ever run by the CCF in Halifax, H.L. MacIntosh, who came very close to winning the seat in a 1947 by-election, was a carpenter who worked in the Dockyard.)

The Local was impressed by the Soviet Union's struggles against Germany and donated at least $300 to the Aid-to-Russia Fund on 16 December 1942 and 5 January 1943. It joined in calls to remove a clause from the union's ritual barring communists, a position that was to be dramatically reversed after the War. It did not, however, protest against the internment of a carpenter incarcerated as a communist during the War, nor did it continue to respond to letters from the National Council for Soviet-Canadian Friendship. In short, Local 83, at a time when the CCF was ahead in some public opinion polls and seemed poised to sweep to power, moved only slightly to the left.

Nor did the Local move very far in the direction of militancy. In 1943, one out of every three trade union members in Canada, at one time or another, went on strike. The members of Local 83 were not among them.

All TLC unions were urged by the federal government not to go on strike, but in the case of Halifax carpenters, many of whom were working directly for the military, even more pressure was applied. There were strikes of carpenters during the war in Nova Scotia, at Debert in 1940, at Point Edward in 1940, and at Liverpool in 1943, but none was serious. Carpenters at H.M.C. Dockyard staged one short walk-out in August 1945 to protest against low wages and the transfer of men to Ontario. The deciding factors in the case of Local 83, however, appear to have been the attitude of its leadership and the concessions made by the federal government. George Smith devoted much time to fund-raising for the war effort (with direct assistance from the Local), for which he was later honoured by being made a Member of the Order of the British Empire. The union came within an inch of striking in 1941, but withdrew from the brink when told by M.S. Campbell, the Dominion Conciliator, that any strike would be illegal. Settlements issued by the Regional War Labour Board were favourable to the Local. The wage settlement of 77¢ per hour for two months and 80¢ per hour after 1 July 1941 was seen by the Local as a very significant victory.

During and after the First World War, labour had been radicalized by the unequal, arbitrary way in which war production and reconstruction had been carried out. During and after the Second, labour was held firmly within the context of industrial legality and its militancy was contained within the ever-widening legal structures of the state. But now came the critical question: would the system of collective bargaining born in the 1930s and extended in the War disappear along with the wartime emergency, or would it continue to dominate the field?

"It is inevitable that an unsettled period will follow after the close of the war unless definite precautions are taken," the Canadian Construction Association had warned in 1940. Events immediately after the War seemed to bear out the prediction.

The immediate postwar picture was one, not of systematic planning, but of chaos and disorder. Severe shortages of production materials seemed to augur a repetition of the economic instability of the last postwar period. On 17 September 1946 the business agent reported that "the principal troubles" facing the carpenters were "the shortage of material, especially nails," and he feared that "if there is no improvement ... men may be unemployed." On 21 Janury 1947, at least 50 men were reported out of work simply for want of building materials; the same month, all the carpenters were laid off at the Bedford Magazine. Local 83 protested to the Minister responsible, C.D. Howe, but was repeatedly frustrated; on 7 October 1947 it voted its heartfelt thanks to the Mayor, who had interceded with Howe as part of a gallant "quest for cement." *The Commercial News* echoed the Local's frustration: "[I]t is not reasonable," it argued in January 1946, "that Ottawa should call for improvement in housing conditions by new construction and refuse the disposal to contractors of a large amount of material warehoused for government contracts which in many cases [was] not used for many months."

The spectre of unemployment also haunted Local 83, as lay-offs at the Magazine and Dockyard combined with a low level of house building. The business agent reported on 4 February 1947: "More Brothers laid off since last meeting. Requested we initiate no more candidates until all now loafing were working." The Local resolved to place an advertisement in the Halifax papers warning all carpenters to stay away "as Employment very bad in City...." By 4 March 1947, 200 brothers were reported out of work; one year later the number of unemployed had grown to 400. The union prepared another "stay-away" notice in early 1949, when over 250 jobless carpenters were reported.

But two initiatives of the federal government, a program to increase domestic housing and a decision to expand Canada's defence system, removed the threat of a general collapse in the construction industry.

One of the first aims of postwar reconstruction was to increase the stock of domestic housing. Critical housing shortages had developed since the slump in home building during the Depression, and the situation had steadily worsened in the 1940s. The improved wages of the latter decade allowed many families to move to larger, separate dwelling units; high marriage rates during and immediately after the War compounded an already critical housing shortage.

The Central Mortgage and Housing Corporation, created in 1945 by the federal government to take over the operation of Wartime Housing Limited and expand the housing stock, was the major federal response to the housing crisis. (George Smith was a member of its board of directors.) While only 59 housing starts were funded in Nova Scotia under CMHC in 1945, just two years later nearly 250 new homes were constructed with CMHC loans totalling $1.35 million.

The postwar drive for more housing changed the relationship of the state to home building, and it also contributed to the erosion of traditional craft methods of house construction. Prefabricated homes for veterans sprouted in suburbia. Some, like D.R. Reay, a lecturer at the Maritime Trade Union Course held in May, 1945, at the Institute of Public Affairs in Halifax, thought that state planning and technological change went together. "While construction can be stimulated by the provision of money at low interest rates and by direct subsidization by the State," he argued, "employment of far more efficient techniques is the only real answer to the problem.... Pre-cutting and pre-fabrication point the way to decreased costs in the future. Through the use of such methods complete integration of the building is now a distinct possibility...." What they might do to the craftsmen he did not mention.

More significant than the resurgence in domestic house building was the development of a boom in institutional and military construction. In 1946, building permit statistics suggest that the division in the industry was approximately $870,000 in housing projects and $1.2 million in commercial building. From July 1949 to December 1950, noted E.A. Saunders in the January 1951 *Commercial News*, "there was an unprecedented boom in Halifax." Building permit estimates climbed from $9.7 million in 1949 to more than $14.5 million in 1950. The major projects in the city included $13 million for new educational facilities, $7.4 million on military contracts, and $5.6 million on waterfront development. After a 60% decline in 1951 to $5.5 million, building permit statistics for the following year suggested an improvement to $7.8 million, with defence contracts adding a further $4 million in new construction. At the time of the strike in 1952, over $25 million in new construction—$18 million defence-related—was delayed. Included in this estimate were the redevelopment of the city's seaward defences, 800 apartment units, quarters for the storage of explosives at the Bedford Magazine, a naval research establishment at Dartmouth, and the expansion of Shearwater. Department of National Defence projects were not confined to Halifax; they provided jobs in many other parts of the province as well, especially Kings County.

The preponderance of government projects prompted the Board of Trade to worry about the implications for the economy of the city. "It would be even more encouraging," it said of the boom, "if a more substantial proportion were industrial construction, representing free enterprise projects that could survive on their own initiative." Others noted that the public works had deepened the divisions between the large and small contractors. Work on large contracts for the Canadian government could only be handled by large contractors financially capable of carrying out such projects, and, according to a spokesman for the Construction Association in 1952, "the smaller contractors are rapidly being forced out of business." The Montreal firm of E.G.M. Cape won the contract for officers' barracks at HMCS Stadacona, while Brookfield Construction seemed to have a remarkable ability to win government contracts, including one in 1951 for a housing development for navy families at Tufts Cove, and another in 1952 for 200 army apartments on North Connaught Avenue. Mechanization itself required capital to meet the extensive costs of replacing worn out or obsolete equipment.

A vivid portrait of the position of the small home builder was provided by B.D. Stevens, who by 1952 had been building homes in the Halifax area for more than 32 years. He emphasized the heavy burden placed on small contractors by the National Housing Act. "We are building houses under the National Housing Act ... almost the first of this type to be built in Halifax for several years," he told the *Mail-Star* on 18 June 1952. "The National Housing Act ... allows a mortgage of about 80 per cent if the selling price is less than $10,000. If the price is above that figure, then the Act says the mortgage must not amount to more than 60 per cent. From our experience in past years we know that most buyers cannot make a down payment of more than 20 per cent, in this case, $2,200. It took us several years to dispose of houses where the mortgage limit was placed at 60 per cent because buyers with the remaining 40 per cent simply were not to be found. The costs of carrying these houses until they gradually were sold, was borne by the contractors." A house worth $10,000 in 1952 (the level the law specified for an 80% mortgage) embodying 2,000 hours of labour had to earn the contractor a profit of $840 to cover the contractor's wages, his cost of getting the business in the first place, and his responsibility for supervision.

This division in the ranks of the employers prompted the formation of a separate Home Builders Association in 1950 and calls for the licensing of all contractors in 1951. Local 83 joined in this call, writing to one alderman in 1948 to demand the enforcement of "licensing of Contractors in City and to make fee larger, with strict examination." (This debate on licensing contractors was destined to go on for more than 30 years.)

One impact of state housing policy was to undermine the craft; yet in other spheres, notably apprenticeship, the state's ostensible aim was to shore up craftsmanship. Nevertheless, apprenticeship shows vividly the two-sided character of industrial legality.

Under the Apprenticeship Act, the provincial government regulated the form of training. Local 83 placed great stock in this new arrangement, and sought to have it extended. Writing to the federal Department of Labour after 1 February 1949, it recommended that "rather than employing helpers at ... Shearwater that they employ apprentices in order to give them a proper training and make good Mechanics." Superintendents of apprentices, such as Harry Grant, tended to be veterans of Local 83. The Local's assistance in having all apprentices in the district attend school was asked for by the authorities. The Local held dinners and donated prizes for successful apprentices, and congratulated the Minister of Labour on his contribution to the program.

But there were other aspects to apprenticeship which were less pleasing. Some carpenters were to charge in 1952 that the Construction Association had shown almost no interest in the apprenticeship project; in that year there were only 41 apprentices, while there were 800 carpenters. The manner in which apprentices graduated from one pay level to the next, based on the number of hours worked, was difficult to supervise. One apprentice who was reported on 27 March 1952 to be working for Brookfield's as a "4,000 hour apprentice," had in fact bluffed his way into the higher pay scale. The biggest deterrent was still the relatively low wages paid to apprentices.

Generally, the postwar period was both a time of accomplishment and a time of reversal. A dramatic change came over the carpenters. Once a small union constantly buffeted by influxes of carpenters from outside the city, Local 83 was now the nucleus of the Brotherhood's organizational efforts throughout the province. Carpenters coming into the city were now members of the Brotherhood, and were exhorted (to quote from the Minutes of 21 September 1948) when they returned "to their various towns ... to see that a Union is formed there." Local 83 was no longer an exclusive craft union, basing everything on limiting entry to its ranks; it was more and more part of an expanding industrial union, basing everything on bringing trade unionism to all who worked with wood. The Brotherhood expanded rapidly in the Maritimes, aided by the organizing efforts of J.H Dwyer, now its main organizer in the East, who paid special attention to woodworking mills.

One insight into the organization of these carpenters in this period comes from a note written by Norris W. Hawboldt, the Financial Secretary of Local 1391 in Kentville, to Leslie E. Wismer of the Trades and Labor Congress. "[O]ur Union was formed in 1949, and the wages in Kings Co., N.S. at that time [were] 80¢ per hour, and now [they are] only $1.10 per Hour, which we have been trying to get raised up to a decent living level, and as far as I can find out, even if we were to get the wage asked in the letter attached, we would still be the Low County in Nova Scotia," explained Hawboldt. "The most of our members work for the Department of National Defence, and for the Contractors who move in and do Defence Contracts, and as the Government cannot sign a contract with the Union, and these Contractors who move in make sure we never get our 55% required for us to urge them to sign a Contract it makes it [awfully] hard for us, and then if we [had] more experience in Union workings, it might be better, but as I said before we have only been going since December 1949, and have not had much chance of learning to[o] much, as Mr. James Dwyer, our organizer, cannot visit us very much, and is kept so busy that if we are able to get him once a year, we are very lucky, and he has helped us a lot, by sending us the Congress Monthly Letters, which [give] us some ideas, and giving us [advice] by letter when we get stuck and write him."[15]

For many of the new members of the Brotherhood, Dwyer *was* the Brotherhood; he organized carpenters from Maine to Newfoundland. George Smith was appointed an organizer for the TLC in December, 1947. Both men were part of a very successful response of the TLC unions to the challenge of industrial unionism, a response which ended with the once distinct strategies of craft and industrial unionism becoming blurred and looking very much like one another.

Part of this new organizing effort was the creation of a new regional level of the union. In January, 1949, Local 1356 of Saint John summoned executive members of Maritime carpenter locals to a conference to see if a Maritime Provincial Council should be organized. At a conference of business agents and delegates in New Glasgow in 1950, they discussed the possibilities of uniform termination of agreements, wages, and the use of the union label throughout the Maritimes. On 2 January, 1951, Local 83 approved the formation of the Maritime Provincial Council of Carpenters. At the first meeting of the Council, dues were set at 4¢ per member per year for construction locals and 2¢ per member per year for mill labour. The Council also resolved that all agreements in the Maritimes should expire on 30 April and last no longer than 12 months. The Council was to encourage the imitation of the Nova Scotia Apprenticeship Act, and vote thanks to the international headquarters for the services of the two Maritime organizers. On 19 June 1951, Local 83 decided to pay 4¢ per year per member to the Maritime Provincial Council of Carpenters, Joiners and Millmen.

The Brotherhood's rapid regional expansion made necessary an intensive effort to define and defend the jurisdiction of the union. The jurisdictional battles with Local 1405 were settled, however adversely from Local 83's point of view, in 1950; those with other unions gained fresh impetus. Local 83 objected to any relations with men associated with the Canadian Congress of Labor (affiliated with the AFL's main rival, the CIO), and pursued a consistent policy of non-collaboration with the enemy. It fought with the painters over the question of carpenters' work on various sites. The advent of new materials sparked new jurisdictional quandaries. Carpenters claimed exclusive jurisdiction over "blown or nailed" insulation, and lathers claimed jurisdiction over all material covered with plaster, plaster board, and other plaster substitutes; both claims gave rise to extensive and often bitter debates. In 1952, the various building trades united behind the reinvigorated Building Trades Council.

Yet this whole series of achievements came at a very high price: in particular, the decline of rank-and-file participation and the centralization of authority in the office of the business agent.

The shop stewards, who had once been the mainstays of the union in the workplace, were no longer a visible presence. The Minutes make only two references to them in this period. On 6 June 1944 the Minutes report a recommendation by the Local, following the request of the business agent, that shop stewards be given 15 minutes instruction by him each month. On 27 August 1946, an executive meeting discussed the formation of shop stewards' councils. "After careful study and consideration," the executive concluded, "it was recommended that Councils were not advisable but that certain duties should be exercised by Shop Stewards such as checking up on new men on a job and to see that dues are kept paid up." These responsibilities were to be embodied in the by-laws of the Local.

The business agent replaced the shop stewards as the principle enforcer of the union's discipline. What was different was not that this collective discipline had to be imposed upon many workers, but that this happened through the actions of one individual instead of through a collective process. In an earlier era, Local 83 had not had a business agent, or it had made do with temporary agents; now to do without the business agent for any length of time was unthinkable.

In many respects the business agent's position was, and is, not an enviable one. He is the labour "entrepreneur" within the labour "business" upon whom the responsibility for the growth and success of the operation ultimately rests. Although he answers to meetings of the Local, these provide at best a loose context within which to work. He not only serves as the major source of the union's information as to events in the construction industry, but speaks for the union in times of crisis; he answers not only to the rank-and-file members he supplies with appropriate jobs, but to the contractors who place the orders. It can be a lonely, frustrating position, whose occupant occupies a difficult middle ground between the rank and file and the contractors. It is perhaps because of the contradictory demands the position makes that some of those who have filled it in Local 83 since 1950 have had difficulty in telling the difference between their personal financial interests and the financial interests of the union.

The permanence and importance of the business agent's position is made clear in references during the War. On 5 March 1940, the business agent was given a mandate to compile a list of those "acting detrimentally to 83," as the minutes so broadly put it; the agent's salary was increased, he was voted a car allowance; he acquired an assistant in 1949 (who for $32.00 per week was to relieve him of the need to keep official office hours), and was bonded in 1952. At the request of the Local, his reports were standardized and those few which survive are long, typewritten documents.

As the emphasis on the Local as a hiring mechanism became more pronounced during the War, the business agent inevitably found himself in a position of authority. On 15 June 1948 we hear the business agent complaining that union men were not reporting to the jobs he had set up for them; on 6 June 1950 it was moved that "the 4 men who refused to accept a job at staging when requested by the business agent, be requested to appear before the Executive and give the cause for refusing this Job." Although the motion was defeated, it suggests the train of the business agent's thinking.

He complained time and again of the haphazard ways of rank-and-file members. After union members had been offered and had refused employment on a job of Maritime Foundation Limited at Cable Wharf, the Local resolved on 20 March 1951 that "the Business Agent be authorized to report any Brother who refuses to accept employment (and he seems fit) to the Unemployment Insurance." (The business agent had two years earlier requested that all carpenters looking for jobs be routed through his office *and* that of Unemployment Insurance.) Two members were charged by the business agent in 1951 for working after hours; they appeared before the union, were given a reprimand, and told on 26 July 1951 that they were to co-operate "in assisting the Business Agent and Local 83 in the future."

The diffuse, ever-shifting nature of the construction industry, responding directly to the business cycle and drawing on a collection of workers that did not have any intrinsic connection with each other, aided the development of this professional form of trade unionism. By the early 1950s, as suggested by the ways in which regional organization evolved, the full-time staff members of the Brotherhood—the business agents, general organizers, and so on—made up its backbone. After George Smith was defeated as president of Local 83 by a close vote of 88-82 on 15 June 1948, there were few figures in the Local who could match their position of authority.

The activities that this greatly changed union undertook, all revealed the impact of the transition to a new style of professional business unionism. There were, in particular, three glaring, significant reversals of previous policies and practices which dramatized the extent of the change: the union's new hall, the way it conducted a major strike, and its shift from the left to the right side of the political spectrum.

The new Carpenters' Building, on Gottingen Street, symbolized the postwar era. A central aspect of business unionism was the rapid accumulation of savings which could be invested in securities. The investment of these savings in an imposing new hall suggested the Local's new strength and confidence.

A good deal of the Local's money came from the Carpenters' Social Club, which was a popular centre for dances and other activities during the War. The Club was financed through shares held by the union, and it returned the proceeds of its events back to Local 83. The Social Club made good money; a total of $16,369.46 in war bonds and a bank account was reported in the 1945 Minutes.

In January, 1950, plans for the new hall, a project with which George Smith identified himself very closely, had become so ambitious that J.H. Dwyer warned Local 83 "not to go very far into debt on this project. Do not put all our eggs in one (building) basket." On 7 March 1950, the 11 provisional directors of the "building committee" were empowered to seek legislation for incorporation under the name of the Carpenters' Building Company of the United Brotherhood of Carpenters and Joiners of America, Local 83, and four months later the Executive voted to invest $40,000 in the new Carpenters' Building. Once the hall was open, the union placed great emphasis on the holding of money-raising dances, organized by the five-man executive of the Carpenters' Social Club set up in October, 1952.

The hall represented the institutional solidity of Local 83, but it also reversed an old pattern. In the period immediately after the First World War, the carpenters had prided themselves on being closely bound with the Labor Party and with other unions, and all these groups had shared the same building. The opening of the hall, at a time when the Halifax Labor Temple had not been rebuilt after the disastrous fire of 1945, was an indication of the Local's greatly diminished sense of belonging to a much broader labour movement, and was of a piece with its demands for a separate building trades department within the TLC and the diminishing presence in the union minutes of news and reports from other unions.

By the early 1950s Local 83 was a powerful, solid, conservative institution. The new hall was an apt symbol of the new attitude towards trade unionism. In the minds of those who had been behind it, particularly George Smith, the union would still serve an educational purpose and the rank and file would be welcome within its walls; they would come in large numbers, he thought, to educational functions and union meetings in the capacious auditorium. The bricks and mortar of the hall represented the union's institutional stability; but they also represented the difficulties in keeping alive the "movement," as Smith unquestionably wished to do, within an institution defining itself more and more as a business.

The same might be said of the 1952 strike, the most dramatic episode in the history of the carpenters in this period. The building trades strike in 1952 reversed an older pattern, in this case that of the similar strike waged in 1919. It thus serves as a useful measure of changes within Local 83 since the first quarter of the twentieth century.

The wide gaps which had opened between the wages of Halifax carpenters and those in other major urban centres in Canada in the 1920s and 1930s were narrowed significantly during the Second World War. Following negotiations during the summer of 1946, building craftsmen were awarded a 40-hour week and an improved pay scale. The *Commercial News* in January 1947 exaggerated when it claimed that skilled building workers in Halifax now enjoyed higher wages "... than in middle and eastern Canada, only exceeded by the border cities of Ontario," but it was right in thinking the enormous discrepancies in wage levels were diminishing in the postwar construction boom. The 40-hour week became something Local 83 doggedly refused to trade away in any negotiations which followed. In 1950, Local 83 won an increase of 15% to come into effect on 1 May 1951, with a further cost-of-living bonus, in a two-year contract. In negotiations in 1951, employers flatly refused to reopen the agreement or discuss adequate drinking water and the condition of shacks at building sites. They insisted on sticking to a two-year agreement. On 11 October 1951, the executive set down 15 demands, the most important of which were: an increase of 34¢ per hour to bring hourly rates to $1.70, four days holiday with pay, and better sheds for carpenters; on 1 April 1952, the recommendation of the Building Trades Council that all unions agree to an across-the-board increase of 50¢ per hour was endorsed. The Construction Association responded with an across-the-board increase of 13¢; it later raised this to 15¢, an offer rejected by Local 83 on 22 April 1952 by a vote of 199 to 81, with three spoiled ballots.

As in 1919, the opening positions were far apart. In contrast with 1919, the issues now had to be referred to a conciliation board, which was headed by Judge K.L. Crowell. The board called for a 17½¢ hourly wage increase, basing its argument largely on the principle that local construction workers should have parity with workers in Saint John, New Brunswick. "In reviewing the wage rates in fourteen of the major cities in Canada, including Halifax and Saint John," wrote Crowell, "it would appear that the average hourly rate of all the building trades in Halifax is considerably lower than in any of the other cities under study. This substantial increase across the board may bring wages in some of the trades beyond what they properly should be in this area. However, it is made with the hope that if accepted by both parties, construction work will not diminish in this area and that happy relations will continue between the Association and the different Unions."

Local 83, which now had about 800 members, rejected the offer of a 17½¢ increase on 6 May 1952, by a vote of 254 to 45 (with three spoiled ballots). On 20 May 1952, 564 members participated in a strike vote: 301 voted for a strike, 259 against. The following evening the Halifax District Building and Construction Trades Council voted in favour of going on strike.

"It is hard to tell how much the strike will affect work," a spokesman for the Construction Association remarked on the eve of the dispute. "It depends on how much control labour has over the workers." The question of how to exert that control preoccupied Local 83 after the third week of May. Ten strike committees were formed on 23 May. The Central Strike Committee warned "all foremen, salaried or otherwise, working on any Building Construction projects [to] leave these jobs immediately."

Over 5,000 men walked out on 26 May 1952. They remained out until 30 June.

As the strike progressed, it turned into a major debate over the direction of the construction industry. According to Russell McInnes, Q.C., in the minority report he wrote as a member of the conciliation board, an 8¢ increase was reasonable under the circumstances. "The Unions admit that production is down," he remarked, "but simply state that there is nothing they can do about it and it becomes evident that the request made by the Union representatives at this time is simply for more money for less work...." He argued that until the unions were willing to set up a system of classification for their own members, the setting of rates for each occupation was difficult.

The unions countered by charging that workingmen were being penalized for the inefficiency of their employers. In an interesting argument, Local 83 put forward the case that one of the reasons for high costs and low productivity was inadequate supervision. "One of the main reasons for insufficient production is ... inadequate supervision on jobs," the Local argued. "Upper Canadian firms would have five supervisors, local firms have one." By keeping wages low, contractors discouraged skilled men from staying in the province. "Many good men leave the province for other centres where pay is higher. Many also take work along other lines." The contractors had had it too easy; they had been getting cost-plus jobs too long, and now demanded too high a profit margin. The result, Local 83 charged, was more and more outside firms underbidding local contractors on provincial jobs. "We're asking for a reasonable living wage," stressed Jack Lynch, president of the Building Trades Council. He noted particularly the huge discrepancy between wages paid carpenters on the East and the West Coasts. As if to underline his point, Victoria carpenters went on strike in the same month for a 50¢ raise from their present $2 hourly rate.

Two things stand out about the case presented by the building trades in the 1952 strike: its sophistication and its business orientation. The sophistication of the unions was suggested when the Building and Construction Trades Council submitted an application to the Department of Labour for a comprehensive public inquiry into all aspects of the construction industry. This was not only shrewd public relations, but it showed also how completely the unions had become immersed in the world of industrial legality.

Meanwhile, new construction worth over $25 million was being delayed, and the Department of Labour looked anxiously for some means of settling the strike.

The strike involved bitter scenes on the picket lines. Some 30 pickets prevented the unloading of a MacCulloch and Company truck near the Kinsac Defence Project in Beaverbank on 30 May. On the Queen's Birthday, only a token guard of three pickets was left on duty at the construction site, and a group of carpenters from Kentville forced past the men and worked. They stopped when 40 more pickets arrived by truck from Kentville. Two strikers were arrested on 16 June 1952 for throwing rocks through a strikebreaker's windshield. Two construction workers, both from Westphal, were convicted of causing property damage and fined on 23 June.

The strike was the first to be dominated by the full-time salaried officers of the unions. J.H. Dwyer was the major Halifax organizer; he was joined by J.O. Renaud, of Washington, vice-president of the Sheet Metal Workers International Union; Harry Calnett, Toronto, of the Painters; J.M. LeBlanc, international representative of the Electrical Workers; Joe Connelly, Toronto, of the Plumbers; and Benedict Tantallo, international vice-president of the Plasterers' Union.

The international representatives and business agents soon had an offer to present—a 15¢ increase. When the offer was put before the men, it aroused intense indignation. In the debates within Local 83, strike committeemen urged the members to go down "fighting as men." The offer was rejected decisively by the Local on 14 June, by a vote of 283 to 82. The strikers then announced publicly that they were ready "for a long siege."

The rank-and-file members and the full-time officials saw the strike in different ways. The representatives stayed in the city and continued meeting with the Department of Labour. On 24 June, J.H. Dwyer addressed a hastily convened meeting of Local 83. His words were blunt. "If brothers turn this down," he warned, "they must be prepared to stay out the rest of the summer." Another representative informed the membership that "this is the final offer, no matter how long we stay out." One worry was the near exhaustion of the contingency fund; most of the carpenters' financial wealth was tied up in their building.

Even after these direct warnings, Local 83 voted against continuation of the strike only by the narrowest of margins, 97 to 90. There was an immediate uproar. At a special meeting called by rank-and-file members, it was charged that the meeting at which the return to work had been approved had unfairly excluded strike supporters because they were unable to leave their picket lines. Dwyer, however, told the men that "it was his ruling that the vote taken last night stands." There could be no question that he was in charge.

After 33 days, the strike was settled at 4:40 P.M. on 26 June, as international representatives of the union and officials of the employers reached agreement at a meeting with the Department of Labour. The strike left carpenters with a rate of $1.51, up from $1.36, but still less than any other construction craftsmen in the city except painters and sheet metal workers, and far below the rates of carpenters elsewhere.

If 1919 represented the triumph of militant craft unionism, 1952 represented the triumph of professional business unionism. The humiliating defeat of the strikers in 1952 was largely the decision of international representatives. Local 83 and other building unions were now much more closely integrated with their respective international bodies. The strike of 1952 brought marginal gains for the workers, but it was experienced more as a defeat, for as a result of all their sacrifices workers came out with a rate that was even 2½¢ below that recommended by the conciliation board, and far below what they had originally hoped to win.

The strike's greatest significance was the revelation it provided into the new forces which were decisively reshaping the Local. Before 1952, the trend to a more conservative business unionism was still open to challenge; after 1952, the die was cast.

In some ways the most striking reversal in the union's position was represented by its shift from the left to the right in labour politics. By 1952 Local 83 occupied a political position diametrically opposed to that with which it had been associated during the pre-war years. Local 83 had been a major centre of left-wing activity in Halifax in the 1920s, and even in the 1930s, under Smith's leadership, it had not withdrawn support from striking unions on political grounds. A more conservative policy began to harden under Dwyer's guidance in 1948. In response to an appeal from Percy R. Bengough of the Trades and Labor Congress on behalf of the Canadian Seamen's Union, Local 83 voted on 4 May 1948 to "lay this communication on the table." Dwyer then "Requested delegates to [the] Trades and Labor Council to support [a] resolution to have Communists, Fascists, etc. evicted from Council...." A debate between left and right opened up within the union in 1948 and 1949. The influence of the left was demonstrated in the protests approved by the Local in 1948 against the expulsion of a left-wing member without trial "for exercising his democratic right to vote at the trades and labor congress," and by objections to the jailing of members of the Canadian Seamen's Union in a strike on the Great Lakes. By 17 May 1949, however, the line had settled: literature from the Canadian Seamen's Union was filed, and an appeal by CSU activists to speak to the Local was turned down, because "owing to pressing business no time could be allotted to a spokesman." (The "pressing business" consisted of discussions regarding the Labour Day Parade.) CSU activists were suspended from the Halifax and District Trades and Labour Council, and Dwyer continued to report to the Local on "the activities of Communists in the area."

The climax came in 1952, when in an ironic reversal of the role it had played in a similar dispute in the Labor Council in 1926, Local 83 gave "whole-hearted approval" to a recent decision of the Nova Scotia Labour Board to refuse certification to five union groups on the grounds they were communist-led. The board refused certification to the Maritime Shipping Federation on the grounds that its Secretary, J.K. Bell, was a communist. (The Board's decision was quashed on 7 May 1952 by the Nova Scotia Supreme Court.) Few other unions took so public or extreme a stand on the issue.

In its institutional life, its conduct of wage negotiations and strikes, and in its politics, Local 83 had changed greatly between 1926 and 1952. The transformation was not quite complete. The automatic check-off of union dues, the intensification of conservatism through the 1950s, and the addition of shelves of labour legislation would take the process much further in years to come. But it was in the Depression and the Second World War—as the union adapted itself to the new world of industrial legality in which it was obliged to function—that the process took firm root.

5

An Ambiguous Legacy
1952-1985

*We refer to construction workers as employees, and in a technical
and legal sense they are. But the relationship between these workers
and their employers and managers is so different from that found in
more stable industrial situations that the use of the term employee to
describe both can be misleading. Because of the very nature of the
construction industry the relationship between employer and employed more closely resembles the simplistic description conveyed by
the expression "labour market" than in perhaps any other employer-
employee relationship. The union, in these circumstances, takes on
the appearance of a labour broker, supplying applicant employers
with the necessary men with the appropriate qualifications....*

*The lack of long-run continuing relationships between employer
and employed in the construction industry has the effect of increasing
the importance of the employee-union relationship. The union, as the
only permanent institution to which the employee can attach himself,
must assume a role in the designing and maintenance of the personnel
policy much more vital than is the case in other industries.*

— H.W. Woods analyzes the modern
construction unions in Nova Scotia[1]

From 1952 to the present the history of Local 83 has been dominated at
every turn by the system of industrial legality and the outlook of business
unionism. The tendencies visible in the years before 1952 became all-
powerful in the years which followed. Before 1952, for all its conservatism,
Local 83 was still a large, working-class institution able to influence the
direction of the local construction industry. Although hostile to inde-

pendent labour politics, its leaders still identified strongly with the labour movement. After 1952, however, the full implications of industrial legality for Local 83 became apparent. Many of the problems facing Local 83 today—declining rank-and-file participation, an increasingly bureaucratic system of industrial relations, the disappearance of a sense of purpose and direction—are hardly confined to this Local. They pertain to the labour movement as a whole. But here they do take a far more dramatic form. The building trades, more than any other sphere of trade unionism, were more radically affected by the new system. After 1952, it became clear that this system entailed, not the adaptation of Local 83 to changing circumstances, but the redefinition of the Local's purposes and methods.

Industrial legality and business unionism undermined the ability of rank-and-file workers to set Local 83's direction. The direction of the industry was determined more and more outside the realm of trade unionism, either through joint labour-management negotiations or through legislation. As the purposes of the union came to be defined strictly in business terms, the operating and financial efficiency of the unit became the primary criteria for most major decisions. First full-time local officers, and finally representatives of the international Brotherhood, stepped in to take over the Local, culminating in the International's imposition of trusteeship. A kind of "building trades separatism," entailing the progressive withdrawal of Local 83 from the other major institutions of the labour movement, followed logically on the decline of a rooted local leadership. The very nature of Local 83 was redefined in the process. Its primary function became the defence of the carpenters' jurisdiction in the labour market, to be maintained through union hiring and to be defended against the persistent claims of the other trades, themselves anxious to encroach upon the jobs claimed by the carpenters. P.J. McGuire, when he helped inspire the founders of Local 83, had seen it as part of a broad and unified labour movement, advancing, step by step, to economic and political power. But by the 1960s and 1970s it appeared to be more an embattled institution, struggling bitterly with other unions for its survival and retreating into isolation before the three threats of technological obsolescence, hostile contractors, and rank-and-file apathy.

The record of Local 83 since 1952 can only be understood if it is placed in its proper economic context—the "building revolution" which transformed the face of Canadian cities in the 1960s and 1970s, and altered the world of the carpenters as completely as did the transformation of production at the turn of the century. This building revolution had two main aspects: the growth of the development industry and the emergence of new building technologies.

As James Lorimer argues in his study, *The Developers*, it was only after the Second World War that land development companies, combining the once separate roles of real estate speculator, property investor, landlord, and builder, started remaking the Canadian city. The policies of the federal government set the pace for this new industry. As it became clear that there would be a large demand for housing after the war, "The federal government decided that it wanted more than just house-builders and houses; it wanted to see a new kind of building industry, with large corporations each capable of producing a sizeable quantity of urban accommodation. The field was no longer to be the exclusive preserve of small-scale independent businessmen as it had been up to the war."[2] The government's Wartime Housing Limited demonstrated that large corporations could effectively build houses, and housing experts argued that the small speculative builder would have to make way for the large-scale producer. Ironically, federal policies, aimed at creating a *building* industry, produced in fact a *land development industry*, making more money from land speculation than from actual building.

But building was not unaffected. Commenting on the corporate development strategy of not increasing the supply of new lots in the face of greater consumer demand, Lorimer remarks, "It helped hasten corporate concentration in the house-building field and the squeeze-out of small builders. The small builders were the last in line to obtain the serviced lots being produced by the large developers when consumer demand for housing was strong. The corporate firms were able to use the existence of a strong market to increase the market share of house-building held by their own house-building divisions and those of the other large developer-builders." In Halifax, he notes, the small house builder's share of the action in building direct-loan National Housing Act units declined from 63% in 1961 to 32% in 1973.[3] Capital in the construction industry was getting much bigger.

Halifax was the construction showplace of the region. In the 1940s and early 1950s defence construction had been the key. Defence remained important in the 1960s, but there was an astonishing boom in industrial, commercial, and residential construction as well. The industrial projects included the vast new Imperial Oil Refinery in Dartmouth (estimated at $25-$30 million) and the industrial parks on the city's periphery. In the 1960s carpenters worked on the new container facility, a new power generating plant, Oland's new brewery on Young Street, and, outside Halifax-Dartmouth, on such large projects as Michelin Tire in Pictou County and the Glace Bay heavy water plant.

Commerical development also proceeded rapidly, with the generous assistance of civic authorities and the CMHC. The area bounded by Grafton, Sackville, Brunswick and Jacob Streets was marked off for urban renewal. (Even Local 83 on 21 March 1950 added its voice to a swelling chorus demanding renovation by drafting a letter to the Premier "demanding immediate action on slum clearance.") An initial emphasis on "social housing" for the area, however, got lost in the rush for profits. The Scotia Square project, which employed hundreds of building workers in the late 1960s and early 1970s, was perhaps the most dramatic symbol of the building revolution.

Although commercial development was reported by the *Canadian Builder* in July 1969, to be "catching up to demand this year in Halifax," this gloomy estimate was soon overtaken by events. From 1974 to 1977 such corporate projects as the Maritime Telephone and Telegraph Centre, the Bank of Commerce, and the Toronto Dominion Bank pushed the total supply of office space up by 50%.[4]

Residential development went forward by great strides. New dwelling starts doubled between 1952 and 1955. Suburbs flourished on the outskirts of the city, and apartment blocks sprouted in its core. Nearly $3 million in military housing was built in the late 1950s. Given the shortage of land on the peninsula, tearing down older structures to provide new apartment sites became the rule, where it had once been the exception.

Apartment blocks began to dominate residential construction. For example, while the total number of new housing starts in 1962 was almost evenly split between single-family dwellings (820) and apartment units (770), during the years 1963-65, 1,800 single and two-family units were built, compared with over 3,200 apartment units. Following a slump in 1967-68, apartment construction in the area boomed again. During the 1969 season, with nearly 1,100 units under construction or near completion, developers planned an additional 1,300 starts for the coming year. A major incentive to residential development, especially in Dartmouth, was the opening of a second bridge across Halifax Harbour late in 1969.

The key to this building boom was the state. All three levels of government were needed for the expansion of the construction industry. CMHC loans to builders were complemented in 1963 by a $500 bonus as an incentive for winter-time construction and by a variety of loans and bonuses. This government assistance in turn put pressure on contractors to reduce labour costs: "Whether builders like it or not," remarked the *Canadian Builder,* "the swing to winter building is on and looks like becoming a permanent feature of our construction industry." It was up to contractors to adopt "new techniques that cut down cost and speed up work despite low temperatures and bad weather." Contractors complained about new levels of state regulation—especially in Halifax, where new by-laws affecting housing density went into effect in the mid-1960s— but they realized that without public assistance the new development industry would have perished. The City of Halifax began a program of tax incentives in the 1960s to spur lagging development projects. Under the scheme, new commercial or industrial buildings would be taxed at 75% of assessed value in the first year following completion; the tax relief would then decline at a rate of 5% per year until, in the sixth year, buildings would be assessed at their full value.

With record levels of construction (building permits at the end of the 1960s broke all previous records at over $100 million) and new patterns of ownership, came an insistence on new methods of production. The range of innovation was almost unlimited. Three major changes stand out: off-site factory production of prefabricated materials became far more common and important; new building materials, such as drywall, plastic, and pre-cast concrete, started to replace wood, stone and plaster; and various types of on-site machinery and equipment, such as power saws, spray painting devices, and large cranes, acquired a new prominence. These three changes, predicted H.D. Woods in an inquiry into the industry in the early 1970s, "may eliminate much or all of the specialized skill components about which the craft unions have been built."[5]

Woods's diagnosis seems confirmed by economic data. When economist Robert Comeau studied the industry in 1965, he noted that carpenters were the largest group of construction workers in Nova Scotia. (They represented about 50% of the province's construction work force, a higher percentage than the national average.) However, carpenters had decreased in numbers relative to other trades quite rapidly from 1951 to 1961. "The requirements for *carpenters* in the industry have been declining for some years and are expected to decline further in the next decade," Comeau wrote. "This reflects the increased use of prefabricated materials and component parts which reduce the number of carpenter hours required on site."[6] The business agent for Local 83 expressed this same thought, rather fearfully, on 18 June 1968: "If the present trend continues," he told Local 83, "the Carpenters on the construction jobs in the future will be very small [in number]. It's time the carpenters realized this and started thinking about connecting trades that are part of the carpentry trade such as Drywall, suspended tile ceiling, aluminum, etc. This might help the Carpenters to work more ... bringing up [their] income and at the same time keeping these trades in the union."

According to a report on the Canadian construction industry prepared for the 1956 Royal Commission on Canada's Economic Prospects, new building products ranged from plywood, plastics and aluminum to the use of structural steel, reinforced concrete, and prefabricated parts. Light-weight concrete became an important component in the new high-rise apartment and office towers. As the *Canadian Builder* noted in July 1964, the construction boom was "rapidly eating into building materials markets formerly monopolized by wood and steel." And as the same journal argued in December, 1969, the most potent reason favouring the use of new building methods and materials was the desire to escape the rising costs of labour. Power trowels, concrete saws, and advanced forming methods were among the many innovations of the age. The 16-storey Spring Garden Apartments (in 1964, the tallest building in the Maritimes) was considered a technical breakthrough in construction techniques such as form work and the more ambitious use of prefabricated materials.

"We have a revolution on our hands," noted the *Canadian Builder* in December 1969. "It is a revolution in management techniques, in methods of building, in the requirements for materials, and most certainly in the market for which we all cater, whether we are manufacturers, builders, architects, suppliers, or engineers." Or, it might have added, the workers who made it all possible.

Whether this "revolution" entailed any long-term gains for labour is doubtful. While it unquestionably meant jobs and wages in the short term, it appears in retrospect to have had three rather negative consequences for local carpenters.

To begin with, the building revolution heightened workers' insecurity without markedly increasing their share of the earnings of the industry. A 1974 study of the building industry prepared for the Economic Council of Canada observed that "In the years since 1966 ... there was only a modest increase in labour's share, as employers partly offset rising per-unit labour costs by substituting more capital intensive techniques."[7]

Carpenters had particular reason to worry about the instability of their jobs and earnings in this period. The same study suggested that "Occupationally, the most striking structural change has been the relative and absolute decline in the demand for carpenters, once the largest single occupational group in construction." It found that in every major city, carpenters' wages had advanced less rapidly than those of other trades, even including organized unskilled labour. In 1951, carpenters in major metropolitan centres came (on the average) within 10¢ per hour of the rate for electricians and plumbers; by 1971, the gap had widened to about 85¢.

Throughout the period 1952-1985, Local 83 navigated in a storm-tossed sea. Jobs were plentiful in the 1950s and most of the 1960s. On 17 August 1965, the business agent "reported the labour situation as improved to the point where at the present time, calls are coming in for men, and sometimes we find ourselves in [a] position [where] we are unable to supply the demand and there were quite a few new jobs opening up." Two years later, on 5 September 1967, he noted that "jobs are being filled as soon as they come into the office," and it looked like the men would be busy right through the winter. By 7 March 1968 the business agent noted a slowing down of work. "Some of the blame is due to members coming back from the outskirts," record the minutes, adding, "It was also noted the Scotia Square and Dalhousie Library are slow in getting started." By 1975, the boom was over. On 18 February 1975, 200 members were reported unemployed; by 3 March 1981, there were 300, and by 6 October 1983, out of a total membership of 800, 270 were looking for work.

Second, the building revolution posed new safety challenges. Far higher buildings meant additional safety risks. These were reflected in a resolution sent by Local 83 in 1956 to the Nova Scotia Federation of Labour, which argued that the large percentage of accidents in the building and construction industry caused by faulty staging, scaffolds and elevators, called out for government inspection and an elevator inspection act. One catches a glimpse of rank-and-file discontent over safety in the brief notation on 7 April 1970: "A few of the Bros. said that there would be more people sick if somebody doesn't do something about the lack of safety on Kenny's job [Fenwick Place] on South St." Many of the so-called "wildcat strikes" during the construction boom were such rank-and-file protests against unsafe working conditions.

Third, and most seriously, the building revolution challenged as never before the carpenters' claims to be highly skilled tradesmen. Other trades challenged their jurisdiction over such activities as form work and the installation of drywall. With a high demand for carpenters as well as relaxed standards of admission, the union faced complaints from contractors that some of its members were not skilled tradesmen. On 5 November 1969 the business agent reported that there had been a number of complaints from contractors, and he added that "Contractors are refusing employment to some of our Local 83 men because of previous time spent with them." On 17 September 1974, the union discussed the "question of unqualified persons posing as carpenters and being sent on jobs," and a week later this problem was said to be one which was "embarassing to the union." How far skill levels declined during the construction boom is difficult to determine. The Local's business agent claimed on 1 October that this problem was being exaggerated. He noted that there were "very few men sent on jobs without proper knowledge of the trade." The general practice, he said, was to send new men to jobs for about 30 days and get an evaluation then made through the employer before they were signed in the union.

One idea, put forward by the Construction Association and supported by some in Local 83, was to compel new men coming into the trade to take an apprenticeship course, and impose tests for the certification of carpenters already in the trade.

There were good reasons, however, to reject certification of the trade. The proposal, it was argued, could easily become a weapon in the hands of the contractors, and it aroused suspicion in the ranks of Local 83. George Smith held on 20 January 1950 that certificates of qualification for carpenters "were a good thing but that we should iron out all the bugs before we sign any contract." Some suspected a disguised wage reduction. As one member argued on 6 October 1959, the Construction Association clearly wanted to "certify just so many carpenters in order to hire the remainder under the regular rate of wage. This would constitute classification, which is something we are opposed to." Meetings between Local 83 and the Construction Association, which came very close to agreement on this issue, collapsed in November 1960. The sticking point for the carpenters was the risk that the Association's scheme of certification would lead to two rates for carpenters. When the issue was raised again in 1956, J.H. Dwyer declared flatly against certification. By 1983, some members regretted the Local's hesitation, for it appeared that the plumbers and electricians, with a certified trade, were able to outpace the carpenters, who were without.

Apprenticeship through the vocational school system continued to function with the Local's blessing. Slowly but surely, however, the building revolution subverted the old ideal of producing well-rounded, general craftsmen.

One impediment was the shortage of apprentices. By 4 October 1960, George Smith reported "that the lack of young men ... taking apprenticeship training in carpentry is serious." The main obstacle was money. An apprentice, starting out with only 50% of the carpenter's wage, and with four years to go, found it very hard to persevere. Apprentices offered more money frequently dropped the course. "A large proportion of those who commence formal crafts training in the vocational high schools and technical institutes cancel before completion of the prescribed course, and of these a good number take employment in the trades and complete their training on the job," Robert Comeau found in 1965. He found that, for the 5,820 registrations in the Apprenticeship Training Program between 1945 and 1965, 1,672 (that is, 34.7%) cancelled before completion.[8] In 1956, according to a report read at the meeting of 5 December, out of 153 apprentices from Halifax to Yarmouth, 30 had been cancelled due to their either moving away or taking up other jobs with more money. Provincial government data also suggested a high drop-out rate. Of 304 carpentry apprentices registered in March, 1970, 95 (31.3%) were in first year, 67 (22%) in second, 84 (27.6%) in third, and just 58 (19.1%) in fourth. Unemployment among apprentices remained over 10% from April 1966 to April 1969, which was worse than the average for the building trades as a whole.[9]

The problems with the apprenticeship system may also have been aggravated by the hostility of employers. Some contractors were reported on 16 October 1962 to be "not cooperating with the apprentices" by refusing to sign their papers or by not hiring apprentices in the first place.

Local 83 found itself without much it could do to improve this situation. Delinquent apprentices were sent letters from the Local "severely reprimanding them and advis[ing] them of the consequences for their negligence," and the Local pushed for interprovincial agreements giving recognition to apprenticeship certificates across the country. But in the absence of mandatory certification for carpenters, apprenticeship continued to play a secondary role to informal training on the job.

Another concern was whether or not the apprenticeship courses were actually preparing young carpenters for the quickly changing construction industry. The Local on 3 September 1967 asked the apprenticeship committee to approach the Nova Scotia Technical Institute to add drywall construction to the methods taught in the course. On 21 November 1972, a report on the Apprenticeship Council argued that the "future of the Carpentry Apprentice is in jeopardy at the present," for general carpentry was in decline and "in future construction will be carried out with men trained for different phases of the job."

By 4 March 1980, radical proposals were aired for the restructuring of the apprenticeship program. Instead of learning the whole range of the trade in blocks, apprentices were, in this new "modular" proposal, to study different phases separately. The apprentice who took framing would study framing, pass an examination, and could then work as a framer. The other phases of carpentry would be open to him if he wanted them.

It was a complete reversal of the old craft ideal of apprenticeship. Instead of producing well-rounded craftsmen who understood the general principles of carpentry, it offered to produce workers who knew one aspect, and who (like workers on an assembly line) would be capable of doing only one small part of an entire job. Contractors were known to wax eloquent about the disappearance of the carpenter who could read blueprints and contribute to the planning of the project. Now the carpentry apprenticeship course made that versatile craftsman even more of a figure from the past. As one member explained on 2 March 1982, regarding a long discussion in the Building Trades Council on modular training, "there was a feeling against this type of training because they will be splitting the trade into specialties." Modular training suited more the interests of the employers buying labour in the open market—who would be assured of a ready supply of most specialized skills—than it met the employment needs of the apprentices, who could easily find themselves unemployed when demand for their particular specialty was soft. But over such objections, modular apprenticeship has become the prevailing mode of formal training.

Apprenticeship is one dramatic example of the changes affecting the carpenters in the mid- to late-twentieth century. Apprenticeship as a rounded education in the "arts and mysteries" of craft was first undermined in the nineteenth century when industrial capitalism eroded such constraints on the supply of labour. The weaker twentieth-century version of apprenticeship, which initially was at least partly controlled by the union and influenced by its ideas of craftsmanship, has since been transformed by the demands of capital for more narrow specialties to meet the requirements of the new technology, and by the state, which now administers the program with only token participation from labour.

From 1952 to 1970 the leaders of Local 83 enjoyed a secure position within the system of industrial legality, while the union was quietly but unmistakably declining all around them. The financial well-being that came with having one's own hall—and the achievement of the check-off, which guaranteed the union a steady income and added to its membership rolls—contributed to a false sense of security.

As the union gained institutional solidity under industrial legality, it placed increasing emphasis on paying off the mortgage on its imposing hall. The financial security it had come to enjoy was suggested by the semi-annual bond report of 20 March 1956. This revealed that the value of the Local's real estate was $125,000; it held $4,500 in bonds and $4,000 in office equipment; in a six-month period it had collected a total of $21,591.76, which was $5,722.37 more than it spent. The Social Club generated a lot of revenue: according to a report filed on 17 November 1959, a total of $54,345.40 was taken in from 257 dances held from 1 November 1958 to 31 October 1959; when expenses were deducted, this represented a profit of $14,014.03. The dances at the Carpenters' Hall became well known throughout the city.

Many of the Local's officers continued in office year after year. In 1965 the Local turned once more to George Smith as president, who, at the age of 71, resumed his old position 17 years after he had first lost it. It was an indication of the union's sense of tradition and, perhaps, the extent to which prosperity had masked the need to respond to economic change with new initiatives.

The trade union structure was dominated, still, by the business agent. (And because the Building Trades Council also employed a business agent who had the authority to sign up members in Local 83, this body was dominated by its business agent as well.) What was said about one case involving a "gypsum job" on 17 October 1952—"Moved & sec Business Agent's action in regards to Gypsum job be endorsed and a free hand be given him in any future action he thinks is necessary"—could be said about scores of others; the business agent *was* the union in the outside world. In one week in 1955 the business agent reported he had placed "125 to 150 Carpenters in jobs in the past 3 weeks...." At a meeting on 18 February 1958, the business agent wanted to know "Just how much authority he has in the way of pulling men off a job"; the Local's revealing reply was that he had the complete power to use his own discretion.

By 1958, it was clear that the structure of industrial legality had made it possible for the business agent to conduct himself rather too much like a free-wheeling labour entrepreneur. Serious irregularities in the receipts filed by him were discovered by the union's auditors. It turned out that some membership money entrusted to him had never been placed in the Local's coffers, and that he evidently had imposed a 10¢ check-off on carpenters working on a job at Mount Saint Vincent University without the Local's knowledge. It appeared likely that this entrepreneurial activity had been going on for some time. On 17 March 1958, he was asked to resign from his post and all other positions in the Local, and it was resolved that a display ad be taken out in the newspapers announcing the end of his time as business agent. Some of the money taken from the union's members was returned to the Local, but the accounts were never fully settled.

Although the episode might have suggested some of the underlying difficulties of business unionism, the natural tendency was to blame the individual involved or the executive members who had been asleep at the switch. Dwyer, now the international representative, took this tack when he informed the members that "the Executive was lax in some of its duties, and that it was the duty of every member to check them." The possibility that the affair might lead to structural, rather than merely personal, changes in the Local was never raised. By 1964, the Local could be seen attempting to restore the same practice—that of initiating men and collecting dues on the job sites—that had proved so disastrous in 1958.

Industrial legality had changed the structures of trade unionism, and we find, in the period 1952-1970, that it had changed union practices as well. Industrial relations procedures became far more elaborate and subtle. Pre-job or mock-up conferences were a key part of the new, far more complicated construction projects. When the Kellogg Company, one of the largest of the new construction firms, undertook a major refinery job, it negotiated with the union beforehand. The resulting project agreement included all the items in the existing local agreement plus the check-off, reporting time, subsistence, commuting time, and a rate for millwrights. The president noted on 16 October 1962 that when they arrived at the meeting, the Kellogg negotiators were "well prepared with all the statistics on labour in general in our area." On 2 April 1963 the Local was told that the meetings with the Kellogg Co. had been a "decided success" with the company conceding the point that all carpenters would be hired from the office with a check-off of dues on the job.

The union's approach to negotiations also became more complicated. On 7 July 1953 the negotiating committee engaged legal council in order to draw up its agreement. While one encounters the old pattern of insisting upon the dismissal of non-unionists from certain union jobs, the check-off of union dues from both members and non-members seems to have taken away some of the urgency of the drive for closed shops. Hiring was now to be regulated—the Local decided on 7 April 1959—by a card system, the introduction of which cost $364.

Perhaps the clearest sign of a new age of trade unionism was the emergence of the jurisdictional dispute as one of the union's main preoccupations. Jurisdictional disputes, rare in earlier periods, now became very common. Two well-documented cases are the disputes with local lathers and labourers.

In the United States, the Carpenters and the Lathers had been battling since 1903. The dispute had its beginning when the Carpenters' General Executive Board signed an agreement giving the Lathers jurisdiction over iron work, including iron or wire lathing. As their part of the deal, the Lathers gave up any claims over all wood work, including shingling, wooden arches, doors or window frames, and wooden studding or furring.[10] The trouble with such decisions—as with all craft unionism in the construction industry—was that new materials and technologies kept messing up such neat jurisdictional boundaries. The two unions fell into decades of jurisdictional squabbling which ended only with their merger in 1979.

Prior to 1952 such complicated international disputes had not affected Halifax workers one way or the other, but now, as international unions tightened their hold on their locals and set their strategies more directly, the defence of jurisdiction became all important. Lathers Local 531 met with Local 83's executive in 1955 to inform the carpenters that they should stop putting on laths, which they were said to be doing on nearly 100% of the jobs in the City. Struggles over which trade had the right to acoustic work proceeded through the 1950s, with frequent appeals for guidance to the General Executive Board. On 17 July 1962 an alarmed business agent "reported the lathers if not stopped immediately would take over the installation of Dry Wall materials." Bro. Dwyer added on 7 August 1962 that "dry wall applications" were "synonymous with carpenters and we should not let the lathers take [them] away from us." Incidents erupted at job sites over the installation by carpenters of metal studs in 1964 and over the installation by lathers of drywall in 1968.

Strenuous battles were also fought with the labourers. In 1959 the business agent was told to investigate reports that the Comstock Co.

allowed labourers to work with carpenters; labourers were also said to be erecting metal forms in concrete in 1961, but when the business agent went to investigate this violation of craft boundaries, "the foremen told him carpenters did not want to work on metal forms but he would put carpenters on there if the local could supply them." On 3 August 1964, "A discussion arose on the increasing number of labourers installing drywall partitions with metal studs, and it was noted that something should be started to have this work brought under the jurisdiction of carpenters." Members of Local 83 who divided their allegiance between the Carpenters and the Labourers were informed they would have to choose one or the other.

At least 30 such jurisdictional incidents are reported from 1952-1970. On the night of 9 August 1969, the business agent outlined disputes with the sheet metal workers over the erection of metal toilet partitions and with the painters over the installation of metal windows. Such jurisdictional disputes were an inevitable consequence of defining unions as labour businesses, for what could be more businesslike than competing with each other for the same labour market? The very large construction sites, quite uncommon before the 1960s, were a jurisdictional wonderland, where clusters of small craft groups competed for influence and members. Even from the perspective of business unionism, this outbreak of jurisdictional squabbling was a disaster, because it gave proponents of compulsory arbitration and other restrictive legislation their best possible arguments. The jurisdictional battles in the 1960s seemed to reveal two limitations of craft business unionism: first, that its craft divisions bore little resemblance to the divisions imposed by modern industry, and second, that its neglect of politics and public image, whatever short-term benefits it may have achieved, was completely counter-productive in the long term.

The political position taken by Local 83 in this period was based more on Cold War emotions than on a realistic appraisal of the Local's long-term interests. Local 83 remained suspicious of labour politics, and opposed the 1956 merger between the Trades and Labor Congress and the Canadian Congress of Labor on the grounds that communists could still be found within the latter organization. While carpenters in Ontario were attracted to the New Democratic Party (and set off a major controversy within the international Brotherhood on the question), Local 83 viewed the founding of the new party without enthusiasm. On 20 May 1958 it resolved that a letter on political education from the Nova Scotia Federation of Labour be "deferred indefinitely" and routinely filed away letters regarding the new party from other locals. Relations with the Nova Scotia Federation of Labour were reasonably cordial—Local 83 voted to affiliate in 1956—but the Local was sharply critical of the Federation's handling of convention resolutions relating to construction.

There was only one significant strike in this period, in July 1970. Some 730 members of Local 83 went on strike against the Nova Scotia Construction Association on 30 July for a new contract; they were joined by 152 members of Carpenters Local 1392, who went on strike against Kenny Construction in Truro, and 450 members of Local 1392, who went on strike against Ellis-Don Co. Ltd., New Glasgow. Labourers Local 615, Sheet Metal Workers Local 409, and the International Brotherhood of Electrical Workers Local 625, also went on strike against the Nova Scotia Construction Association. (In August they were joined by the International Operating Engineers Local 721.) Given the emphasis later given to the alleged "turbulence" of industrial relations in Nova Scotia construction in these years, it should be emphasized that this was a large, but completely legal and peaceful, strike. The violence associated with construction disputes elsewhere in the country was not characteristic of the region. A strike for higher wages was virtually inevitable considering the magnitude of the building boom; what was surprising, perhaps, was how peaceful labour remained. Some measure of the booming conditions of construction in the city can be gained from a partial list of the projects closed down in the strike: the life sciences and performing arts buildings at Dalhousie, Scotia Square, Fenwick Towers, the container terminal, J.L. Ilsley School, and the Dalhousie Arts Centre. As early as 4 August 1970 (according to the *Mail-Star*), the carpenters indicated they were willing to talk with the Association, but spokesmen for the Association refused to do so, because they suspected the carpenters only wanted to negotiate offers the employers had already rejected. The strike ended on 21 August with a very favourable settlement: a new contract calling for a $1.70 per hour increase over three years (bringing the hourly rate by 1 November 1972 to $5.05).

Yet despite steady progress on wages and despite financial stability, members of Local 83 had a sense that something was very wrong with the union. On 18 October 1954, Lloyd Hennigar, a veteran unionist, remarked that "the local is in an unhealthy condition" and that he "would like to know where the trouble lies." Membership meetings no longer contained the fiery debates of old; they now tended merely to confirm the decisions taken by the executive. Many members who paid initiation dues in order to retain their jobs were so indifferent to the union that they did not appear for initiation. Others quietly dropped out, causing Hennigar to remark, "there should be some thought given to the reason why so many members are dropping out of the union."

Attendance at meetings was at its lowest ebb. George Smith, who had done so much to build the modern union, was shocked. On 6 June 1961, he said "it was a terrible thing to look around the hall and see so few members present," even while a new contract was being negotiated. Two weeks later, the secretary noted that at the meeting called to elect the executive, only 72 members out of a possible 832 showed up.

From 1963 to 1965 the membership of Local 83 declined. It was estimated on 31 March 1964 that a minimum of 950 members was needed to operate and maintain the Local; it had about 743. In January 1965 it sank as low as 623. In 1965, after a long examination of the crisis, the executive recommended the hiring of an assistant business agent. It suggested advertising meetings on the radio. On 3 June 1969, a visiting organizer from New Brunswick remarked that "the work in the Halifax & Dartmouth area has been on the increase for some time and so has the amount of carpenters working, but the membership of the local stays the same. It's about time this local took some interest in organizing." Union carpenters were shut out from most work in the residential part of the industry, the business agent reported in 1968. Dwyer spoke candidly of the "lack of confidence of some of our members."

It was a paradox: a union with such a long tradition and such institutional strength seemed to be weakening during a time of economic boom. Part of the problem lay in the relative powerlessness of the average member, who rarely saw an executive decision overturned or an incumbent challenged for office. (Many elections of this time went by acclamation.) Business unionism, truly, did not require an active mass base. Older craft unionists such as George Smith, who still saw Local 83 as a movement which needed an actively participating membership, were dismayed by this turn of events, and placed their hopes for recovery in persuading a large number of carpenters to take an active part. Others, like J.H. Dwyer, thought that media coverage of labour was to blame, and hoped that the trade union movement would undertake a campaign to restore public confidence. But the remedies that ultimately were applied to the Local's mounting crisis of membership and finances were to steer it on an opposite course.

From 1970 to the present Local 83 has been transformed by two revolutions in the construction industry. The building revolution of new techniques and materials has continued to menace the trade with the spectre of obsolescence, and when the building boom finally ended in the mid-1970s, there was a marked decline in the demand for carpenters. But a second, possibly more serious, revolution has also taken place. This legal revolution has tightened a close web of statutes, regulations and committees around the construction unions, and (although its architects never presented its potential impact in this way) has completed the work of industrial legality started in the 1930s.

Interpreting so recent and important a change is difficult, for a number of reasons. It is difficult to assess the very recent past with the same objectivity one brings to more distant events. In this case, much of the evidence is conflicting and has not yet come to light. The whole question of the making of modern law in the construction industry is immensely complex, as commission follows upon commission and statute upon statute.

Yet some fairly basic points can be made about this process, and about the underlying positions of capital, the state, labour, and the new labour specialists. Since many of these basic points have been lost in the often complicated and biased presentations of this new "legal revolution," it is worth our while to summarize them here.

The impetus behind the rewriting of construction labour laws in the 1960s came from business and the state. When business considered its position in the construction industry in the 1960s, it worried that it had lost ground with labour. It naturally wanted to buy labour power at a price lower than that demanded by the workers, and it looked to the law to make sure that the construction and development booms of the 1960s and 1970s kept generating the enormous profits to which it had become accustomed.

This was not quite the way the business point of view was presented. Rather, spokesmen for business argued that construction, as a particular form of economic activity in which many trades combined to produce the finished product, needed special legal treatment. This was so particularly because of two strategies adopted by unions: "leapfrogging" and "whipsawing." Leapfrogging was a method used by unions when one employer had to sign an agreement with several locals. One union could wait until a trend of settlement had been established, and hold out for a better deal. It would probably win, because the cost of a high settlement with one trade would probably not appear too great compared with the cost of delaying the entire project. The holdout union thus gained a considerable advantage over those which settled quickly. Whipsawing, on the other hand, meant that when one union or a group of unions dealt with several employers, they exerted unequal pressure on competing employers by singling out one or more favoured contractors and letting them continue at work. Possibly they would reach an agreement with the contractors whose work had been allowed to continue, under which the latter would abide by any agreement made by the union with other employers. The union could then exercise its full bargaining might against other employers, who had every incentive to settle. The tactic was effective because the union's direct pressure was supplemented by the additional pressure of having a competing firm take all the business.

The combination of these two tactics was said to have created an imbalance of power in favour of the unions. When such writers as H. Carl Goldenberg and John Crispo examined construction labour relations in the 1960s, they argued that trade-by-trade bargaining and leapfrogging were of fundamental importance, and that the only way around such problems was a gradual centralization both within and between trades of bargaining practices in the industry. One way to do this was to impose a legal accreditation scheme on the contractors in a given area, which would oblige them to deal with unions through one association.[11]

From the perspective of the state, imposing some form of discipline upon labour during a construction boom was an important goal. Many of the largest building projects, such as the heavy water plant in Glace Bay, involved public money, and prolonged labour difficulties could be politically embarrassing. Others, such as the Michelin plant in Pictou County, while technically "private," were in fact almost as "public," because they were central to the provincial government's new development strategy. In Nova Scotia, the suggestion that outside capital might be frightened away by labour militancy carried a great deal of weight, and protecting the province's public image was one of the government's key interests.

Labour's position in this equation was ambiguous. As Brian MacLean observes in an important essay on labour-management relations in Nova Scotia in the 1960s and 1970s: "It seemed that something dramatic had to be done to stimulate expansion of union membership. The province had more trade unionists in 1943 than it did 20 years later. The labour members thought that expansion of union membership depended on labour's public image." Acceptance of the legitimate role of labour by management spokesmen would help offset a negative image of trade unions.[12] A srike in the Hants County gypsum fields evidently forced some trade unionists to believe that a legislative remedy was necessary if labour rights were to be acknowledged. The potential critics of such a policy had largely disappeared in the 1950s, a time of extreme conservatism in the labour movement. And some of the more ambitious labour leaders could not have found it unpleasant to rub shoulders with the province's major industrialists and be treated, if only momentarily, as social equals.

The role of a new group of industrial relations intellectuals in transforming the situation of construction unions should also not be overlooked. These "labour relations experts," operating from the Institute of Public Affairs at Dalhousie University, had inherited a position of influence from the old Maritime Labour Institute, and they saw the construction industry in Nova Scotia as an important testing ground for a number of theories. Industrial harmony, the prevention of strikes, was at the centre of their thinking. Industrial conflict was not, for them, an inevitable aspect of an industrial capitalist society; rather, strikes and other disputes arose mainly out of faulty communications, which it was the duty of industrial relations experts to repair.

In their outlook and tactics, the industrial relations intellectuals resembled rather closely a group, active in England in the early twentieth century, called the Fabians. Like the Fabians, the Institute of Public Affairs intellectuals stressed the value of planning, efficiency, and order, which could all be better served through the achievement of bigger and more broadly based bargaining structures. Sector-wide and multi-trade bargaining appealed deeply to them. Also like the Fabians, they pursued a strategy of permeating the upper echelons of the labour movement with their ideas. Uninterested in building a movement for a new labour philosophy from the bottom up, they concentrated instead on working from the top down, by recruiting a select and very discrete group of labour leaders and businessmen who would share their interest in promoting labour harmony.

The central body in which this brave new world of industrial relations was to unfold was the Nova Scotia Joint Labour-Management Study Committee (JLMSC), which became famous throughout the country. It won praise from both *Industrial Canada*, the organ of the Canadian Manufacturers' Association, and from Joe Morris, then vice-president and later president of the Canadian Labour Congress. It emerged in response to a call by Judge A.H. McKinnon, serving as a one-man fact-finding commission on industrial unrest. McKinnon wanted Nova Scotians to consider the benefits of adopting European, and particularly Swedish, approaches to industrial relations, which emphasized voluntary consultations between labour and management. The JLMSC, which brought the leaders of trade unions, important industrial figures, and intellectuals together, was a voluntary advisory group whose influence on local labour legislation was considerable. It was based on the commitment by labour and management that neither would propose changes to the Trade Union Act, but that all such proposed amendments would go through the JLMSC. "This meant that possible changes in legislation that might be designed to facilitate labour-management relations in the construction industry would require Study Committee investigation—*unless* the government of the province undertook to initiate such changes without labour-management consultation," writes C. Roy Brookbank, a prominent proponent of the new approach.[13]

The history of the legal revolution and the JLMSC's role in shaping a new role for construction unions is shrouded in myth, for its architects have understandably been concerned to present the best possible case for it. While Nova Scotia's labour legislation is generally backward and repressive, and has lagged behind the rest of the country, the myth presents it as one of the most advanced bodies of labour law in the country. While the industrial disturbances in Nova Scotia in the years leading up to 1962 were generally pretty minor—the decade of the 1950s was the quietest in twentieth-century Nova Scotian labour history—the proponents of the JLMSC liked to portray the province as they found it in 1962 as a turbulent, class-divided place, crying out for the calming influence of Dalhousie professors.

This whole story needs to be looked at again. At least as far as construction goes, one comes away with the image of a complicated but effective propaganda offensive. Basically the Construction Association outmanoeuvred labour, and emerged from the process with most of the reforms it wanted. The intellectuals emerged with a large number of titles to add to their resumés. The government built its big projects, some of them new monuments to its short-sightedness. And labour emerged with new restrictive legislation, a reputation for political compromise to live down, and a steadily weakening position in the economy.

This new philosophy of labour-management harmony made its first impact on construction with a 1964 report by law student Peter Green, supported by a grant from the Nova Scotia Department of Labour and organized by the Industrial Relations Section of the Institute of Public Affairs (and funded, one might add, in small part by Local 83, which greeted the new labour-management scheme with quite a bit of enthusiasm—although doubts were expressed about adopting too much of the centralized Swedish model). Green's report emphasized the differences which characterized the construction industry and suggested that the Trade Union Act should take these differences into account.[14] An Advisory Committee of employers and union leaders, which assisted in the collection of data and influenced the direction of the investigation, continued to function after the report was published, and became the first Construction Industry Subcommittee of the Joint Labour-Management Study Committee.

In 1968, a far more influential report, commissioned as a Centennial Project by the Canadian Construction Association, was released by Dr. H. Carl Goldenberg and John H.G. Crispo.[15] This privately commissioned report was a sign that the construction industry, more quickly than labour, realized that survival in a system of industrial legality meant obtaining political clout through persuading people with detailed arguments.

Goldenberg prescribed a number of tough measures for construction unions. He wanted special recognition for the industry in labour law, the continuation of the collective agreement in the event of employer merger or succession, better administrative machinery for jurisdictional disputes, and a Canadian counterpart of the AFL-CIO Building Trades Department in the United States to settle the same disputes. The heart of the Goldenberg Report, however, lay in four core recommendations: multi-trade bargaining, binding arbitration to replace strikes for the settlement of grievances, new powers to issue "cease and desist" orders for Labour Boards or, if necessary, the Supreme Court, and finally the certification of most bargaining units on the basis of geographical area. These recommendations were backed up by extensive evidence. They constituted a major assault on the power and position of the trade union movement.

In 1970, the Nova Scotia government, prompted by a number of small strikes in the construction industry, brought in H.D. Woods, an industrial relations expert, to recommend changes in the Trade Union Act. But for the new labour intellectuals and construction industry spokesmen, Woods was a disappointment. Although he did recommend some of the kinds of centralization and reorganization favoured by Goldenberg, throughout his report was a sense of the basic fact that labour and capital, representing different interests, were bound to struggle with each other. The government might moderate this conflict, but it could not eliminate it.

Here the Woods Report clashed with the underlying orientation of the JLMSC. In a case where the parties were renegotiating an expiring agreement the suspension of the strike or lockout was to be lifted automatically with the expiration of the agreement. In a case where recognition was voluntary and no collective agreement was in existence, the suspension of the strike or lockout was to be lifted one month after the parties had jointly requested conciliation services, or one month after they had notified the Construction Industry Panel that collective bargaining had commenced. Finally, in the case of bargaining where certification had been issued and where no agreement between the negotiating parties was in existence, the suspension of the strike or lockout was also to be automatically lifted one month after the notice to commence collective bargaining had been given.[16] Woods thought there was a continuing place for the strike or lockout: "Industrial conflict is inevitable in our society simply because there are conflicts of interest in the employment relationship," he argued. "They will continue ... A society which faces some industrial turbulence because of full employment is in better economic and social health than one which faces the defensive turbulence created by fears arising because of underemployed labour resources."[17]

The responses to the two reports were very revealing. Even though the Goldenberg Report was privately commissioned by, and reflected the underlying interests of, the Construction Association, it became the Bible of the industrial relations experts, while the Woods Report, with its realistic grasp of power in industrial relationships and its more reasonable assessment of why workers went on strike, was politely ignored. The Goldenberg recommendations, writes Brookbank, became the yardstick "against which subsequent progress towards more effective construction legislation in Nova Scotia can be measured."[18]

On 6 July 1971, the provincial Liberal government of Gerald Regan enacted Bill No. 1, otherwise known as the Construction Project-Labour Management Relations Act, and proclaimed it for Pictou County. This specified that collective agreements be settled between construction employers and the majority of trades involved in a project before the project was undertaken, and that any disputes related to negotiations connected with the projects be settled by compulsory arbitration. The allocation of work between trades was to be decided at pre-job conferences between employers and unions. This represented a major challenge to the JLMSC, because the government had introduced new labour legislation without first consulting that body, and it also revealed the extent to which it would rewrite the statute book to oblige Michelin, whose plant construction at Granton, N.S., the law was designed to facilitate.

In the 1930s and 1940s, industrial legality had appeared to workers, not altogether incorrectly, mainly as a way of protecting themselves in the labour market. Now the negative side of formalized industrial relations became much clearer. The government, by clever manipulation of labour laws, could effectively challenge a union's right to organize, and imposed upon the construction workers of one county a special law from which other workers were excluded.

This became painfully evident on 14 June 1973 when the provincial government introduced an Order-in-Council to make two critical changes in the regulations under the Trade Union Act. One made it virtually impossible for the Labour Relations Board to certify a craft union in an industrial plant. (Could it have been a coincidence that the International Union of Operating Engineers was, the next day, about to appear for a hearing on an application for certification at Michelin?) The second changed the regulations regarding certification votes. Both these changes posed grave threats to the JLMSC because they had emerged as law without first having been discussed by that committee.

The government's major intervention in the construction industry came with the amendments to the Trade Union Act in 1972. As Brookbank notes, the Nova Scotia Trade Union Act of October 1972 embraced "all of the most significant recommendations put forward by Carl Goldenberg, H.D. Woods, and the Nova Scotia Joint Labour-Management Study Committee."[19] There were four major changes. The legislation provided for the formation of a Construction Industry Panel as a section of the Labour Relations Board, speedier certification, accreditation of an employers' organization as sole bargaining agent for employers in a given geographical area, and provision for arbitration as the final step in dealing with grievances arising during the life of a collective agreement. The major breakthrough was clearly accreditation of employers, which fulfilled one crucial element in Goldenberg's prescription. (The provisions for conciliation and arbitration indicated, on the other hand, how little affected the government was by Woods's acceptance of the strike as a legitimate aspect of industrial relations.)

Inside Local 83, the 1972 Act aroused some scepticism. One top union official remarked on 21 March 1972 that accreditation would prevent contractors outside the Association from dealing with the union to hire men during a strike, and any contractor certified by the union would automatically come under the jurisdiction of the Nova Scotia Construction Association. "This," he said, "is like having the Union organize members for the Construction Association." The labour leadership in general viewed accreditation by sector as a step ahead, and in such unions as the carpenters' the boundaries of the Locals were changed in response to the new scheme. Other unions, however, were worried about the impact the new arrangement would have on their national agreements, and fought the Construction Association Management Labour Bureau Limited, now organized to represent accredited employers, all the way to the Supreme Court. The Bureau was finally accredited for the mainland of Nova Scotia on 28 January 1976.

There is reason to doubt the assumption that accreditation was the universal boon the industrial relations intellectuals said it was going to be. In 1974, the employers, to fight against a strike by various trades during collective bargaining, locked out other, non-striking trades. By exerting equal pressure on all construction unions, whether they were on strike or not, they in effect adopted a version of the strategy of whipsawing. Trade unionists who still wished to bargain on a trade, rather than a multi-trade basis, were now obliged to bargain on the employers' terms. "The use of the lockout undoubtedly curtails the freedom of individual trade unions to use the strike as an economic weapon, " Brookbank admits, although he adds, "but it also brings about better coordination in collective bargaining and greater stability through coordinated settlements."[20] What it rather appears to have done is transfer the advantage of bargaining in construction from one side to the other.

And has accreditation, in exchange for this substantial loss of freedom within the local unions, provided the better coordination and stability Brookbank describes? In 1974, James E. Dorsey wrote an important study on the question of accreditation which took up this very point. "Theoretically, increased stability in construction labour relations will accompany accreditation," he argued. "Accreditation, however, will be accompanied by a greater opportunity than ever for employers to agree to illegal combinations. It may cause collusion between labour and management, thereby increasing inflationary trends in construction. It will probably be accompanied by a growth of non-union firms and greater employer resistance to unionization. All of these factors point to the conclusion that accreditation will add to, rather than decrease, the instability of construction labour relations."[21] Eleven years later, as contractors face the decision whether or not to go "double-breasted" (that is, form a non-unionized double of their unionized company), and trade unions face the menace of a growing non-union sector, Dorsey's prediction seems to have been borne out.

Accreditation and most of the other aspects of the legal revolution have made democracy within the trade union movement much less likely. Surround a trade union with complex, intricate regulations which require weekly consultations with lawyers; centralize bargaining authority in province-wide bodies dominated by full-time professionals; and create powerful joint labour-management bodies whose decisions are, for the most part, taken without reference to rank-and-file opinion—and you have assembled all the ingredients for bureaucratic unionism. This problem was never considered by the industrial relations intellectuals, yet the withering of rank-and-file participation was probably the most significant development stemming from the legal revolution they so enthusiastically championed.

The emergence of accreditation as the panacea for which local trade union rights should be sacrificed was an example of a narrowly defined economic interest group, the Construction Association of Canada, gradually imposing its view on a wide range of industrial relations experts and even labour leaders. Yet the core arguments for its view were never really solid. They tended to be based on two rather dubious assumptions. One was that just as certification was necessary for unions in the bargaining relationship, so too should accreditation be necessary for employers. But there are fundamental differences between groups of employees and groups of employers. One is, as Dorsey suggested, that employees in a group have roughly equal economic strength and share common interests, while employers have different economic strengths and conflicting interests. Another, more fundamental, difference is that while employers have a wide array of weapons to use in the bargaining situation, from formal lockouts to simply withdrawing from the field, employees have only a few, and labour law has severely restricted their use.

The second dubious argument was the allegation that a serious imbalance had developed between unions and management. But the case for a serious imbalance of power in favour of the unions was never substantiated. The construction unrest in Nova Scotia in the 1960s and early

1970s was a normal response to a sudden labour scarcity, much as the unrest in 1919 and 1952 had also reflected increased demands for construction labour. "Industrial relationships operate in an economic context and there is a feeding of influence from the conditions of the labour market into the relationships between employees and employers and unions and employers as well," argued H.D. Woods. "Thus, economic growth is taken as a desirable goal for Nova Scotia where unemployment has been high by national standards and underemployment is also a matter of concern. Yet it was the increased volume of investment in large scale operations which had much to do with the turbulence in the construction industry. In a real sense the solution to some of the unemployment problems created industrial relations disturbances."[22] Evidence of turbulence and disorder in the Nova Scotia construction industry in this period is far from impressive. Taking the most visible example of construction labour unrest, only 13,600 worker-days were lost at the heavy water project, from 1965 to 1967, less than 5% of the total worker-days available, and far less than one finds in many single strikes in industry. A lot of this unrest stemmed from resentment of a supervisor on the project and a badly botched industrial relations strategy by the contractors.[23]

What happened was that the momentary bargaining strength of labour on these big construction projects was interpreted, by advocates of accreditation, as a permanent imbalance of power. But the balance of power is not set in stone. As Dorsey observed, the question of which party in construction labour relations, at any given time, can assert the greater power "is very much dependent upon whether there is a high demand for construction or a high rate of unemployment in the industry."[24] And as George Bain, an industrial relations expert, asked in 1971, "If accreditation legislation is introduced now to correct a power imbalance which is presently in favour of the unions, what is to be done when the balance of power moves in favour of employers? Is the accreditation legislation to be repealed, or is additional legislation increasing the power of unions to be introduced?"[25] That, perhaps, is the critical point to be faced in the present time of labour's defeat, and one upon which the labour relations experts have been strangely silent.

Local 83's recent history suggests the continuing difficulties of business unionism within this context of industrial legality. Since the early 1970s, the Local has been unable to organize carpenters effectively.

Until 1983 the business agent continued to hold the most important position in the Local, but his role became increasingly difficult and controversial. Some sense of his authority, and the distance between the office and the membership, emerges from a case reported on 1 June 1971 in which a member was charged with using abusive language to the business agent and office staff and fined $20. The business agent on 27 May 1970 was informed that because of his attitude towards a change in office routine, his lack of interest, and his refusal to cooperate, he was being reprimanded and told either to do the work assigned to him or to step down. On 15 March 1971, another business agent was hired, but not permanently, because none of the candidates seemed sufficiently experienced and "the very existence of Local 83 depends on the right leadership." The successful candidate soon developed business interests, first joining Industrial Estates Limited as a labour advisor, and then resigning in 1974 to take up a position with the Northdown Drywall Company. His successor was persuaded to resign by the Brotherhood's international representative, and the next office-holder was removed in January, 1985, on the grounds of irregularities in his receipts and of failing to administer the hiring system so that each member was given a fair shot at the going jobs. In response to this series of difficulties, the Local gave consideration in 1985 to making the position of business agent an appointed one. This would reverse a 50-year-old tradition.

The Local's activities have declined. Often only a few members turn out for meetings. When Gerald Yetman of the Nova Scotia Federation of Labour addressed the Local on 16 April 1974, he remarked that "One of the things that was most noticeable was the lack of attendance at our meeting." In 1982, Local 83 initiated a door prize of $20 to tempt members back, but by 7 February 1984, only six members were present at a regular meeting out of a total membership of 817.

The Carpenters' Social Club ceased to operate on 16 March 1976; the club had been declining over the previous few years, and attempts to rejuvenate the business had been to no avail. Although the Local continues to receive large sums of money, it must also spend a great deal on fighting grievances and on its mortgage. To alleviate a perceived financial difficulty in 1982, the Building Company looked into the possibility of selling the Carpenters' Hall at 2015 Gottingen St. The hall is itself symbolic of the changing fortunes of the Local. Conceived by George Smith as an important social and cultural centre for labour, the auditorium of which was to be used for educational and other activities, the Hall is now largely rented out to other tenants. The auditorium is used mainly for bingo and a pornography shop occupies the ground level.

The Local has been changed in recent years into an organization representing carpenters from Halifax to Weymouth. New Glasgow Local 1392, which had jurisdiction over Kings and Hants Counties, informed Local 83 that it could no longer service these areas and suggested it would be willing to cede control to Local 83. Local 83's executive recommended that Local 1392 be offered $1,800 for the jurisdictional rights, itself an interesting reflection of business unionism. By 1979, Local 1392 itself was reported in financial trouble and Local 83 considered absorbing its members. The merger of Local 392, Liverpool, and Local 83 was reported imminent on 25 September 1984. The result of these developments is a Local which now represents a very diverse and scattered population of carpenters. And the membership of this geographically extended Local was smaller in October 1983 (800 members) than it had been at any time since 1970; this can only represent an absolute, sharp decline in its Halifax membership.

Although Local 83 passed a resolution on 21 May 1974 in favour of Canadian autonomy within the Brotherhood, the International has come to play an ever more direct role in its affairs. In 1977, a representative from Head Office attended Local 83's meeting and presented a letter assigning him to review every aspect of the Local's operation. By 23 November 1982, another visitor from the International addressed the executive, and informed them that he was present to investigate reports regarding "negligence that is taking place in the local." He had intended to place the Local under trusteeship, but delayed this decision for three months to permit local men to correct the negligence. On 1 June, 1983, the international representatives were reported as having brought about the resignation of the business agent.

The Local was placed under suspension, which meant that its capacity to make decisions was severely limited by the Brotherhood. On 8 January 1985, the international representative reported on statistics he had accumulated concerning Local 83 over the past months, and noted that generally "production is not what it should be." The Local is now directly controlled by the Brotherhood.

The new industrial relations system places priority on negotiations at the top levels, and Local 83's participation in such negotiations is now secondhand. Multi-trade bargaining in these negotiations has also aroused controversy. On 1 June 1973, "Bro. Smith reported there is considerable controversy with the idea that all trades would bargain together. He said the Plumbers & Electricians . . . prefer to bargain separately and it seems that one is trying to outdo the other in wage scale." The difficult multi-trade bargaining of 1980 left some bitter feelings in the Local. On 7 October 1980 the Local resolved "that we look into the legalities of sending a letter to the Construction Bureau re: the recent agreement signed by the Electricians & Plumbers . . . and if we have no response then we would have it publicized." Multi-trade bargaining achieved from below, as in 1919, could unite crafts, but that imposed from above seems only to divide.

Another consequence of the new legislation has been to deepen the rift between the building trades and the rest of the labour movement. One finds as early as 20 July 1971 the remark, "One of the things discussed at meetings of construction trade unions was the lack of cooperation by the Nova Scotia Federation of Labour representatives. It is felt by most representatives of trade unions that [the] Federation does not want to get involved when construction trades unions have problems." By 1 April 1980, Local 83 resolved that the Provincial Building Trades Council would be the official voice of construction "when it comes to legislative action with the N.S. Government." Intense displeasure was expressed inside Local 83 over the rough reception given Gerald Regan at the 1976 convention of the Nova Scotia Federation of Labour, and over the NDP's activities in the local Labour Council in 1972. Local 83 viewed without enthusiasm the rise of rank-and-file militancy in the 1970s. Preparing on 1 September 1970 for a debate over the Canso fishermen's strike at the convention of the Nova Scotia Federation of Labour—a debate which was short-circuited—delegates from Local 83 were reminded "that if the question of the Fishermen's Strike at Petit de Grat comes up then they should voice their opinion against any union that is communist led or inspired, as stated in our own constitution." Given this background, the national building trades split with the Canadian Labour Congress in 1981 over the voting rights of building trades unions, and the founding of the Canadian Federation of Labour in 1982 (on the platform that the CFL "cannot be politically partisan and do a proper job of representing the union movement") did not represent too sudden a split from the rest of the labour movement for Local 83.[26] If the CLC launches serious raids on the building trades the energies of trade unionists shall, to an even greater extent than in the 1960s, be focussed on fighting each other. Once the cornerstone of the Halifax labour movement, Local 83 is now in isolation.

The damage done by the split between labour centres may be less, however, than that done by a union claiming much the same territory as Local 83. Much of the carpenters' jurisdiction is being lost to the Labourers International Union. On 25 April 1979, the Minutes noted that "It's apparent that the Labourers are doing more of the staging as time goes by. Both the B.A. and Representatives from Head Office [say] that we must get this work under the jurisdiction of the Carpenters as it can mean many hours of work for carpenters." Although the two international unions made an agreement in 1982 that each would not include the skills of the other in its training program, this did not end jurisdictional conflict. On 25 July 1984, Local 83 was told by a board member that the challenge from the Labourers had grown even more serious. Labourers Union Local 183 was said to be training its members to be form carpenters, making a drive to take over all form work in high-rise buildings from the carpenters.

The most vivid sign of the Local's deteriorating position and the new world of union politics was the South Shore/Valley Zone Agreement, concluded between the Construction Association Management Labour Bureau Limited and Locals 83 and 392 of the United Brotherhood of Carpenters and Joiners of America. This 1984 agreement covered the counties of Lunenburg, Queens, Shelburne, Hants, Kings, Annapolis, Digby and Yarmouth. The agreement's preamble noted the extremely difficult conditions faced by the unionized sector of the construction industry, and noted, "[T]he Bureau and the Union are agreed that the unionized sector of the construction industry must adopt extraordinary and aggressive means to become more competitive in the South Shore/-Valley Zone." The hardship clause would redefine a normal work day as consisting of ten hours of work payable at straight time, Monday through Friday inclusive. Further, it was agreed that up to eight hours of work on Saturday were to be payable at the shift time rate.

This ten-hour agreement was debated extensively in 1984. On 3 July, "There was a long discussion on the 10 hr. agreement that was made with the 'form' Contractors. It was explained the agreement was made after numerous meetings with the 'Form Contractors' over their not being able to compete with non union contractors because of the difference in wages. The contractor[s] want to stay 'union' but they are being forced to go 'double bre[a]sted' in order to get the tenders accepted."

It is understandable that the ten-hour agreement, whatever its background in the economics of the industry, should have caused quite a heated debate. It represented rolling back the achievement of the nine-hour day, something the carpenters won first in 1889. Carpenters in 1912 considered but ultimately rejected the proposal to admit ten-hour millmen to the ranks; now carpenters in 1984 faced the same problem, but were forced to come to a different conclusion.

On 17 July 1984, the general representative from Head Office spoke to an unusually large meeting of Local 83. He told the carpenters the agreement had been made with the form contractors after many meetings. "He said the contractors were looking for concessions to the present agreement that would enable them to be competitive when tendering against non union Companies. He went on to relate some of the conditions across the country of the unemployed union carpenters and some of the drastic changes that have taken place with other local agreements in order to keep their members working. . . ." After a "very heated ¾ hr. debate" the Local rejected the agreement by a vote of 40-13.

However, on 25 July 1984, a board member from Head Office spoke to the Local on the ten-hour question. The employer had phoned the Brotherhood's Head Office, and the heat was on Local 83. "He said the General President was called by the General Form Contractor in this area over the refusal of the members of the local to accept a change in the agreement. He said the proposal of the 10 hr. day was a fair change in the agreement considering the position the contractors are in. He said other local union[s] are making concessions to their agreement[s] because they realize that tough times are ahead and they will have to bite the bit until times get better."

He then informed the Local that, however much it protested, it had no right to block the agreement. "He said that this Local is still under suspension. He said the Executive has been making some progress but ... [the general international representative] is still assigned to this local. He said a letter will be sent to the local instructing them on what decision has been made re the 10 hr. work day, that has been proposed."

From the viewpoint of the advocates of the ten-hour agreement, the union is fighting for its life. From the viewpoint of the agreement's critics, the acceptance of ten hours in a "hardship clause" in one agreement is likely to start an unfavourable trend to longer hours in construction in general. The ten-hour agreement emerged because Local 83 feared that the contractors in the Bureau would "go double breasted"—forming parallel, non-union companies—unless they got some concessions in the building trades agreements. Unless this process was stopped, Local 83 could be driven out of existence. The balance of power now clearly resided with the contractors, and non-unionized hours and wages were becoming industry standards.

The hundredth anniversary of the affiliation of Local 83 with the United Brotherhood of Carpenters and Joiners of America thus takes place at a time of serious internal and external difficulties for the Local.

Internally the carpenters face the challenge of restoring some local democracy, so that ordinary members of the Local once again feel they have some power. If Local 83 is once again to be a dynamic labour union, it will have to enjoy far more control over its own affairs. The centralizing trends of provincial labour legislation and the Brotherhood will have to be reversed, and the years of Local 83's isolation from the rest of the Halifax labour movement left behind.

Externally the challenges are even greater. The expansion of the non-unionized sector, the menace of technological obsolescence, the weakness of the union in the residential sector, and the rivalry of other construction unions, all pose tremendous problems for Local 83. Its survival can lie only in surmounting them.

The most critical challenge now facing Local 83—and Canadian trade unionism in general—is to recover a sense of social purpose. Business unionism, which turned against labour politics and a vision of labour as part of a broad struggle for social justice, now finds itself unable to motivate unionists to undertake the hard task of rebuilding the labour movement.

The carpenters find themselves in the same position as their ancestors of the early twentieth century. Just as the carpenters of 1912 had to rethink many aspects of the craft tradition, the carpenters of 1985 now are faced with an equally difficult appraisal of the customs and habits of decades. They too must wrestle with the dilemma of preserving their position in the industry by allowing members to work ten hours a day. Just as the carpenters of 1912 had to come to terms with the ambiguous legacy of craft organization, so too do the carpenters of 1985 have to ponder the equally ambiguous legacy of business unionism and industrial legality. The carpenters of 1912 dealt with the problems which confronted them by building strong alliances with other unions and turning to labour politics. How the carpenters of 1985 will face their own more serious challenges is a question for the future.

Notes

Preface

1. R. H. Tawney, "The Conditions of Economic Liberty," in *The Radical Tradition* (Harmondsworth, 1964), p. 117.

Chapter One

1. On P. J. McGuire, see Walter Galenson, *The United Brotherhood of Carpenters: The First Hundred Years* (Cambridge, Mass., 1983); David N. Lyon, "The World of P. J. McGuire," unpublished thesis, University of Minnesota, 1972; Robert A. Christie, *Empire in Wood: A History of the United Brotherhood of Carpenters and Joiners of America* (Ithaca, N.Y., 1956). The high cost of McGuire's itinerant life-style is suggested by the fact that only after he returned from this speech in Halifax did he learn that his wife had died in his absence, on 26 January, 1884. The Amalgamated Trades Union passed a motion of sympathy, and made McGuire an honourary member.
2. See Eugene Forsey, *Trade Unions in Canada 1812-1902* (Toronto, 1982), pp. 184-197 for a survey of Canadian building unions in this period.
3. For an outline of this early Society, see C. Bruce Fergusson, ed., *The Labour Movement in Nova Scotia Before Confederation* (Halifax, 1964), p. 11; the rules may be consulted in the *Rules and Regulations of the Brother Carpenter Society* (Halifax, 1833). In some sources, this Society is cited as one of the early, if not the earliest, Canadian trade unions, but I have yet to see any firm evidence that it acted like a trade union, assumed such trade-union functions as bargaining over wages, hours, or conditions, or that it ever led strikes.
4. Susan Buggey, "Building Haifax, 1841-1871," *Acadiensis,* Vol. X, No. 1 (Autumn 1980), pp. 90-112; see also her "Building in Mid-Nineteenth Century Halifax: The Case of George Lang," *Urban History Review,* No. 2 (October 1980), pp. 5-20.
5. Cited in Galenson, *op. cit.,* pp. 76-77.
6. See, for example, Robert Q. Gray, *The Labour Aristocracy in Victorian Edinburgh* (Oxford, 1976), among many other titles.
7. See Public Archives of Canada (PAC), MG 28, I 265, L3:1892:P, Reel #M-6557, Proceedings of the Seventh General Convention of the United Brotherhood of Carpenters and Joiners of America, p. 14.
8. Richard Price, *Masters, unions and men: Work control in building and the rise of labour 1830-1914* (Cambridge, 1980), Chapter 2.

Chapter Two

1. Nolan Reilly, "The Emergence of Class Consciousness in Industrial Nova Scotia: A Study of Amherst 1891-1925," Ph.D. Thesis, Dalhousie University, 1982, and also his "The General Strike in Amherst, Nova Scotia, 1919," *Acadiensis,* Vol. IX (1980), pp. 56-77.
2. Canada, Commission of Conservation, *Fire Waste in Canada* (Ottawa, 1918), illustration between p. 146 and p. 147.
3. PAC, RG 27, Vol. 32, Files 1-3, "Special Investigation in regard to the tendency of the Rates of Wages and Hours of Labour in Canada, The Building Trades."
4. Robert Christie, *op. cit.,* p. 196, notes that the Brotherhood was more interested in "policing" woodworking than in "organising" it.
5. Public Archives of Nova Scotia (PANS), RG 7, Vol. 382, No. 203, Arbitration Award of 1903.
6. The Brotherhood as a whole grew from 68,400 to 200,700 members from 1900 to 1910 (Galenson, *op. cit.,* p. 122).
7. The Halifax Minutes are silent on the question of the big strikes of 1909-11, in contrast with the records of Local 452, Vancouver, which are said to make many references to support given the equivalent coal miners' strikes on Vancouver Island. See Carpenters' Pensioners' Association, *Building British Columbia ! The Story of the Carpenters' Union and the trade union movement since 1881* (n.p., 1979), p. 21.
8. For the general context, see Craig Heron, "Labourism and the Canadian Working Class," *Labour/Le Travail,* Vol. XIII (Spring, 1984), pp. 45-76.

Chapter Three

1. Department of Labour Library, Canada, Royal Commission on Industrial Relations, Minutes of Evidence (microfilm), Reel 4, pp. 4418-4419.
2. PAC, Records of the Department of Labour, RG 27, Vol. 302, file 13 (63).
3. PAC, RG 27, Vol. 303, file 14 (17).
4. Wayne Roberts, "Artisans, Aristocrats and Handymen: Politics and Unionism Among Toronto Skilled Building Trades Workers, 1896-1914," *Labour/Le Travailleur,* Vol. 1 (1976), p. 103.
5. Minutes of Evidence, Royal Commission on Industrial Relations, Reel 4, p. 4415.
6. *Ibid.,* p. 4359. There is a description of Dane in Clifford Rose, *Four Years with the Demon Rum* (Fredericton, 1980), pp. 5-9.
7. PANS, MG 20, Vol. 525, No. 1, Minutes of the Executive and Management Committee, Halifax Relief Committee, Minutes of 15 February 1918.
8. *Ibid.,* 20 February 1918, interviews with Watters of the TLC and John W. Bruce of the Plumbers.
9. *Ibid.,* 5 August 1919.
10. Gregory S. Kealey, "1919: The Canadian Labour Revolt," *Labour/Le Travail,* XIII (Spring, 1984), p. 39.
11. The general background is presented by Anthony MacKenzie, "The Farmer-Labor Party in Nova Scotia," M.A. Thesis, Dalhousie University, 1969.
12. John Manley, "Communists and the Canadian Labour Movement During a Period of Retreat: The 1920s," unpublished paper presented to the North American Seminar, Dalhousie University, 1979, p. 26.
13. Galenson, *op. cit.,* p. 212.
14. *Ibid.,* p. 300.

15. Selig Perlman, *A Theory of the Labor Movement* (New York, 1928), pp. 188-189.

Chapter Four

1. See Laurel Sefton MacDowell, "The Formation of the Canadian Industrial Relations System During World War Two," *Labour/Le Travailleur,* III (1978), pp. 175-196.
2. Cited in Galenson, *op. cit.,* p. 106.
3. Leo Panitch and Donald Swartz, "Towards Permanent Exceptionalism: Coercion and Consent in Canadian Industrial Relations," *Labour/Le Travail,* XIII (Spring, 1984), pp. 133-157.
4. H. A. Logan, *State Intervention and Assistance in Collective Bargaining* (Toronto, 1956), pp. 26-27.
5. PAC, RG 66, Vol. 13, file H-4-32-S1, J. C. Beattie to W. M. Dickson, 23 September 1936.
6. PAC, RG 66, Vol. 13, file H-4-32-S1, Gordon B. Isnor to R. O. Campney, 16 August 1938 (copy).
7. PAC, RG 27, Vol. 106, file 424-02:36, J. C. Beattie to Norman McL. Rogers, 23 September 1938 (original); also RG 66, Series E, Vol. 13, file H-4-32-S1.
8. PAC, RG 66, Series E, Vol. 13, file H-4-32-S1, memorandum of National Harbours Board, 25 November 1938 (copy).
9. PAC, RG 27, Vol. 106, file 424.
10. PAC, RG 27, Vol. 106, file 424-02:36, Mrs. Marie Dean [of the Mackenzie King Club] to Ernest Lapointe (copy), 14 October 1939.
11. PAC, RG 66, Series E, Vol. 13, file H4-32-S1, J. C. Beattie to R. O. Campney, 23 June 1939.
12. PAC, RG 66, Series E, Vol. 13, file H4-32-S1, J. C. Beattie to Norman A. McLarty, 20 August 1941 (copy of telegram).
13. PAC, RG 66, Series E, Vol. 13, file H4-32-S1, Gordon B. Isnor to R. K. Smith, 21 August 1942.
14. Thomas Raddall, *Halifax: Warden of the North* (Toronto, revised edition, 1971), pp. 274-275.
15. PAC, MG 28, I, 103, Canadian Labour Congress Papers, Vol. 1, File: 1-15, Carpenters and Joiners of America (Part II), 1947-1956.

Chapter Five

1. *Report of the Commission of Enquiry into Industrial Relations in the Nova Scotia Construction Industry* (n.p., mimeo, 1970) [Woods Report], pp. 16-17.
2. James Lorimer, *The Developers* (Toronto, 1978), p. 16.
3. *Ibid.,* p. 117.
4. *Ibid.,* p. 164.
5. Woods Report, *op. cit.,* p. 20.
6. Robert L. Comeau, *Manpower Requirements in the Construction Industry of Nova Scotia* (Halifax, Economics and Research Division, Department of Labour, 1966), p. 66.
7. Economic Council of Canada, *Toward More Stable Growth in Construction* (Ottawa, 1974), p. 64.
8. Comeau, *op. cit.,* pp. 74-75.
9. Economics and Research Division, Nova Scotia Department of Labour, *Nova Scotia Apprenticeship Statistics 1970* (Halifax, 1970), p. 10.

10. See Galenson, *op. cit.,* pp. 362, 116-117, 214, 340-341 for details.
11. H.W. Arthurs and John H.G. Crispo, "Countervailing Employer Power: Accreditation of Contractor Associations," in H. Carl Goldenberg and John H.G. Crispo, eds., *Construction Labour Relations* (Ottawa, Canadian Construction Association, 1968), pp. 376-377; and "Summary and Conclusions," pp. 648-670.
12. Brian MacLean, "Nova Scotia Labour and the Joint Labour-Management Study Committee, 1962-1975," unpublished essay, Dalhousie University, 1979.
13. C. Roy Brookbank, *Legislative Changes in the Construction Industry in Nova Scotia 1965 to 1975: An Exercise in Industrial Democracy* (Halifax, Institute of Public Afairs, Occasional Paper No. 2, 1977) p. 4.
14. See Peter G. Green, *Labour-Management Relations in the Construction Industry* (Halifax, Institute of Public Affairs, 1965).
15. H. Carl Goldenberg and John H.G. Crispo, eds., *op. cit.*
16. Woods Report, op. cit., p. vi, Recommendations.
17. *Ibid.,* pp. 133-134.
18. Brookbank, *op. cit.,* p. 10.
19. *Ibid.,* p. 19.
20. *Ibid.,* p. 23.
21. James E. Dorsey, *Accreditation in Construction Labour Relations* (Halifax, Institute of Public Affairs, Discussion Paper No. 74-01, 1974), p. 44.
22. Woods Report, *op. cit.,* p. 133.
23. See the *Report of I.M. MacKeigan, Q.C., Industrial Inquiry Commission Respecting Deuterium Construction Projects Glace Bay, Nova Scotia* (1967), p. 42.
24. Dorsey, *op. cit.,* p. 32.
25. Cited, *Ibid.,* p. 33.
26. See the Canadian Federation of Labour, *Position Papers* (n.p., 1982), p. 1.